The Beach Boys' Endless Wave

The Beach Boys' Endless Wave

Inside America's Band

by Rushton 'Rocky' Pamplin
and Ron Hamady

Westcom Press
Culver City, California

Copyright © 2018 by Rushton Pamplin and Ron Hamady

Printed in the United States of America

All rights reserved. No part of this publication may be reproduced, stored in any retrieval system, or transmitted in any form or by any means, mechanical, photocopying, recording or otherwise, without permission in writing from the publisher, except by a reviewer, who may quote brief passages in a review.

Published by Westcom Press, LLC
10736 Jefferson Boulevard, Suite 383
Culver City, CA 90230
westcom.press@mac.com

ISBN: 978-1-938620-24-9 Hard Cover
       978-1-938620-22-5 Paperback

Library of Congress Control Number: 2018943560

Cover Design by Chris Flynn, Flynn Creative
              www.FlynnCreative.com

Front Cover Photo –Getty Images

To Beach Boys fans—
You make the music possible.

TABLE OF CONTENTS

Acknowledgments ix
Introduction: Call Us The Guardian Angels 1

Section I: 1976-1977 5

Chapter 1 Laughs and Hoops 7
Chapter 2 Last Ditch Effort 17
Chapter 3 A Day in the Life 31
Chapter 4 Owoooooo! 45
Chapter 5 The Troubadour 57
Chapter 6 It Must Be the Squab 63
Chapter 7 Wipeout 73
Chapter 8 Brian's Back 81
Chapter 9 A Year into Our Gig 89
Chapter 10 Brian's Christmas Gift 95
Chapter 11 Barefootin '97 103

Section II: 1978 113

Chapter 12 Dirty Deeds Down Under 115
Chapter 13 Close Call 129
Chapter 14 The Soundcheck... 137
Chapter 15 The Showdown 143
Chapter 16 Fame and Fortune.. 157
Chapter 17 Celebrate Like There's No Tomorrow 163
Chapter 18 Betrayal... 171
Chapter 19 I Love You 177
Chapter 20 No Thanks.. 187

Section III—1979 and Beyond 191

Chapter 21 California Feelin'.. 193
Chapter 22 Wheaties—What The Big Boys Eat................ 205
Chapter 23 We Lose Dennis 209
Chapter 24 Mike and the Prince 219
Chapter 25 Europe.. 225
Chapter 26 The Camel Man 239
Chapter 27 Thanks! 249
Chapter 28 You Know It's True—Brian's Back 255
About the Authors 261

Acknowledgments

For the time of my life in the Seventies and thereafter I thank The Beach Boys and all those involved with making them America's Band.

Introduction

Call Us The Guardian Angels

I had the privilege of spending two-and-a-half years imbedded, behind the scenes, with the enormously talented Beach Boys' family.

Mike Love and his younger cousin Brian Wilson started the Beach Boys in the early Sixties and co-wrote the string of hit records that gave the group the undisputed title of "America's Band." Mike was front man and lead singer; Dennis and Carl, Brian's two younger brothers, and their good friend, Al Jardine, drummed, strummed, and harmonized their way to stardom. Mike's younger brother, Stephen, helped manage the band for years, finally becoming the band's full-time manager in 1972.

Along with Stan Love, the youngest of the three Love brothers, I began to work for Brian and his wife Marilyn in 1976, a pivotal year in Brian's career. Brian hadn't traveled with the band for well over a decade. Though he had stopped touring to focus on creating new music, he sank into a deep spiral of drug abuse and the music stopped after only a few years.

The Beach Boys stayed alive on the back of Mike Love's charismatic lead singing and hard-working stage presence, becoming widely respected for their constant touring and great concerts. Still, they weren't firing on all cylinders without Brian and they needed him back in the fold with them.

The Beach Boys wanted Brian functioning, writing music, and touring again to keep their franchise as America's Band from fading in the hugely competitive world of popular music.

Though the Beach Boys needed Brian, he was not in any position to help them. His situation was dire.

Brian's out-of-control drug use had irretrievably damaged his nervous system, he was about to be institutionalized, and he was in danger of dying. When his manager and cousin, Stephen Love, came up with a last-gasp alternative solution and presented it to Brian's wife, Marilyn agreed. Thank God!

Stephen asked his younger brother, my former college roommate Stan Love, to move in with his cousin Brian and live with him and his family 24/7. Stan was quickly joined by other members of Stephen's team, one of whom Brian dubbed "Honest Injun" (no one knows why, but that's Brian for you). When it was

As good friends and roommates at the University of Oregon, Stan Love (right) and I were looking forward to being stars in the NBA and NFL. We ended up on a worldwide roller-coaster ride with the Beach Boys.
Photo by and courtesy of Sandra Ficalora

clear that even more help was needed, Stan invited me to join the team as well. Stan and I quickly became the core members of the team, charged with the incredibly important and difficult task of reversing Brian's downward spiral.

Stan and I were former pro athletes in our twenties, well-known for partying and having a pretty good time ourselves. Despite our well-earned reputations, Stephen had unwavering faith in our ability and desire to protect Brian—we became his guardian angels. Stan had always adored his older cousin, and I grew to love the quirky, sweet, and remarkably funny guy as I spent hours with him in his house, in the gym, at the recording studio, and on tour.

We took our charge soberly and seriously, and we did our damnedest to live up to Stephen's standards. You may have read Brian's recent memoir, I am Brian Wilson, or Mike Love's Good Vibrations: My Life as a Beach Boy. This book fills in some of the missing links in the extraordinary story of the Beach Boys and their phenomenal, endless wave of success.

Section I:
The Comeback, 1976-77

Chapter One

Laughs and Hoops

It was a typical southern California afternoon—sunny, just a tad smoggy, with a refreshing offshore breeze that made it delightful to be outdoors.

Stan Love, my best friend and former college roommate, led me inside Brian Wilson's sprawling Bel Air mansion to grab some Cokes. Stan is Brian's younger cousin, and he'd recently become his chief protector.

He had prepared me for a shock: I wasn't going to meet a clean-cut, smiling Beach Boy, but a huge, shaggy, paranoid schizophrenic.

We went in the front door, through the two-story formal foyer and past the spiral staircase, past the lavish living room, done in vintage antique décor, including a nine-foot Steinway concert grand piano, covered with dozens of family pictures in an assortment of beautiful frames. We passed a formal dining room with a table for twelve and walked into a state-of-the art kitchen.

The kitchen overlooked a gigantic tree-lined backyard and a gray slate patio area with a sunken Jacuzzi and an enormous mosaic tile lined swimming pool.

My head was on a swivel, unable to fully take in all the eye-catching opulence of the world-renowned Beach Boy's family home. We made our way back to the beautiful mahogany-lined office just off the foyer, but not before peeking into the enormous family room complete with high-tech entertainment center, including the biggest television I'd ever seen. I couldn't get my head around "Brian's Beach," a bizarre indoor sandbox with a magnificent white baby grand piano plopped in the middle.

Brian was deep into his daily routine, nothing but smoking and pacing from one end of the house to the other and back again. Stan had told me that Brian did this over and over for hours at a time, and he said I needed to ignore it.

Brian's slide into this manic state began well over ten years before at the peak of the Beach Boys early fame. They had a number-one album, a top ten hit, and were on tour when the pressure seemed to overwhelm Brian. He suffered a nervous breakdown on an airplane just before Christmas 1964 and left the tour, swearing he'd never go on the road again.

Brian wrote some of the best music of his life over the next two years before discord within the band and his rapidly escalating drug use short-circuited his goal to surpass the Beatles. Without music in his life, Brian's downward slide escalated; his mental and physical state had bottomed out when Stephen came up with his plot to save him. A plot that I was about to join.

We settled into the office with our Cokes just before Brian wafted by in a cloud of second-hand Marlboro smoke. He was barefoot, wearing a crimson pair of drawstring bell bottom pants and a matching t-shirt with *The Wizard* stenciled in gold across the front.

Stan and I carried on a casual conversation, a conversation we had completely fabricated the night before and rehearsed for hours over a couple of beers and some laughs. We knew Brian would overhear us as he walked back and forth in the quiet house. Since he was usually averse to formal introductions as part of his laid-back, casual, California-cool style, he would have a no-pressure option if he wanted to meet the person with whom Stan was chatting.

Here's the bare-bellied Brian Wilson, all 311 lovable pounds of him, that Stan and I hauled out of bed after he spent a decade lying around stoned and stuffed.

*Photo by Stan Love
from the Larry Salisbury Collection*

After making a few circuits, Brian surreptitiously peeked into the office as he went by. He could see Stan, who was sitting behind the oversized mahogany desk, but he couldn't see me as Stan and I talked about some made-up good old days at the University of Oregon.

Stan purposely projected his voice; he knew our friendly chitchat about wild parties and wilder girls might pique the interest of a Beach Boy who had a year at a local community college and had never gone away to school.

After a few more eavesdropping passes by the office, getting an earful of our adventures at raucous college parties, Brian couldn't resist the temptation; he had to know with whom Stan was having so much fun reminiscing. Without missing a beat, he just slipped into the office and walked to the desk. Never looking my way, he interrupted with, "Hey, Stan."

Stan barely paused. "Hey, Brian." He continued our conversation, throwing the verbal volleyball back into Brian's court. Brian feigned interest in the books on the mahogany shelves, still not looking my way, unwilling to appear the least bit curious with whom Stan was shooting the breeze about fraternity parties and the chicks they had screwed.

Behind Brian's back, I said, "After I boinked her, I put on the white t-shirt I had been wearing that had her scent on it, lit a cigarette, said I had to pee, excused myself, and said I'd be right back. I left the pitch-dark bedroom, closed the door, and gave the scented shirt and cigarette to a fraternity brother. After a couple of minutes, he flushed the toilet and went into the bedroom, took a last drag off the half-smoked cigarette, put it out, took off the white t-shirt, climbed into bed, and he gave her a really enthusiastic round two."

I remind you that this is all a made-up ruse, a raunchy story Stan and I rehearsed the night before in the hopes we might break through Brian's shell.

Brian laughed along with Stan but still wouldn't look in my direction. I continued my story, "After the second guy finished doing the unsuspecting girl, he said he needed to pee again, and explained, 'It must be all the beer.' He put on the white, perfumed t-shirt, lit a cigarette, left the bedroom, and handed the t-shirt and half-smoked cigarette to a third fraternity brother.

He followed the pattern, flushed the toilet and re-entered the bedroom, put out the cigarette, took off the shirt, and climbed on for round three.

Brian laughed again.

"The girl was surprised, and when she said, 'You sure are horny,' the third guy said, 'Well, I haven't been laid all day!'"

This sent Brian into a laughing, coughing jag. Stan was laughing too, and he patted Brian on his back and offered him some of his Coke to drink.

I continued my phony story. "Guy number two and I were listening outside the door, and when we heard number three say he hadn't been laid all day, we couldn't help cracking up. When she heard us laughing, the girl shrieked, 'Who's that?'"

"Number three said, 'How should *I* know? I've been with you all night.'"

Brian and Stan were rolling with laughter, and Brian finally begged, "Stop! I'm gonna pee in my pants!"

The three of us lost it. The story was mean and not even that funny, but we were in the throes of contagious laughter.

Brian rushed to the bathroom, calling out, "I peed my pants!"

At that point, Stan and I almost peed, too, we were laughing so hard. Stan yelled to Brian, "We're going outside to get some air."

Brian shouted back, laughing, "Are you *sure* you didn't pee in *your* pants?"

At this point, anything and everything was funny. We were in sync, and the three of us had started the bonding process.

As Stan and I made our way down the long walkway at the front of the estate, we heard the amplified voice of a celebrity tour bus guide, paused in front of Brian's mansion, announce,

"This is the home of Beach Boy Brian Wilson. He and his cousin Mike Love are the musical geniuses who wrote the legendary hit songs such as 'Surfing USA,' 'California Girls,' and 'Good Vibrations,' just to name a few, that southern California is renowned for." The bus slowly moved away as the tourists gawked, took pictures, and pointed their fingers, exclaiming in unison, "*Wow!*"

Stan knew that Brian's wife, Marilyn, was due home any minute, so he said, "Let's shoot some hoops out back by the garage." He took his shirt off and told me to do the same. We had warmed up and were glistening with sweat when Marilyn drove up in her classic chocolate brown Mercedes Benz SL convertible. She braked and unabashedly stared at Stan and me. After getting herself a good eyeful, Marilyn pulled up and parked.

Stan told me to continue shooting hoops and went to open Marilyn's door, giving her his best playful smile. "Hi, Marilyn. Here, let me help you with your packages."

As he retrieved them from the trunk, he noticed Marilyn peeking in my direction. "Oh, hey, that's my friend Rocky."

She blushed shyly and smiled at me. "Hi."

I smiled back with a friendly "hi."

When Stan and Marilyn turned the corner at the side of the chauffeur's quarters and were out of my earshot, Marilyn stopped Stan. "Who's *that*?"

"That's my roommate from college. He was the star football player at Oregon."

Marilyn remarked to herself, "He looks familiar." It took a beat before she recognized where she'd seen me. Then she stammered, "Hey, ah, wasn't he a *Playgirl* guy earlier this year? He was on the cover and . . . ah . . . um . . . in the nude. I mean, he's a centerfold, right?"

"I wouldn't know—*I* sure don't read *Playgirl*."

Marilyn giggled, "No one does. We just look at the pictures."

Inside the house, after Stan unloaded her packages, Marilyn asked, "Would your friend like to stay for dinner? I'm going to order take-out from the Luau on Rodeo."

"Well, I don't know; I'll have to ask him. He has a very active social life."

Marilyn grinned. "I'll *bet* he does."

"You should have seen how he had Brian laughing earlier."

"Really!" Marilyn exclaimed. "Brian never laughs. He barely even talks."

"Well, Rocky made him laugh so hard he peed his pants."

She laughed, "You're kidding! Brian peed his pants?"

"Have Brian fill you in."

"I will."

Stan came back out and filled me in on his conversation with Marilyn. He even re-enacted the "Who is *that*?" scene and her excited mention of my Playgirl centerfold. He added, "Marilyn invited you to dinner."

"I've got a date—but I'll break it."

"Man, you made a great first impression on both of them."

That evening the four of us had fun, joking and laughing at dinner. Well, three of us did; Brian ate quickly, then left us to lie down on the couch.

Life had been tough for Marilyn for the past few years. She'd married Brian when she was a 17-year-old singer with her own band, two years after she met Brian at one of his gigs. Brian had been on his downward slide into drugs and mental illness during most of their marriage, and she was raising their two daughters (then six and almost eight) pretty much on her own. She was only 29 years old and she appreciated the chance to laugh and have some adult conversation. After dinner, she extended an invitation to me to come over for dinner any time, and said, "Any friend of Stan's is always welcome."

That night Stan called his brother Stephen and told him about my first meeting with Brian and Marilyn. Stephen was the Beach Boys' manager, and it'd been his idea to hire Stan to keep Brian away from drugs and get back into shape.

Stan described how well we hit it off, and he suggested Stephen should talk to Marilyn about hiring me to help with the demanding and challenging task of rehabilitating Brian from his drug addiction.

"I could use him up here, and between us, we could get Brian more physically involved, maybe even join in with basketball. Brian really took to him. He'd be perfect. Brian's choice of Honest Injun wasn't going to be enough."

Stephen agreed, adding, "Sounds like Marilyn might even like the idea."

The next day, he broached the subject with Marilyn. She agreed. "I think that's a great idea, Stephen. Brian really liked Rocky. And I think Stan could use a competent hand to assist him. It's a much bigger job than we originally thought."

The Love brothers offered me the job over dinner; I was all in, as long as I had some flexibility to audition and act in commercials.

"That's not a problem," Stephen assured me.

We quickly agreed upon terms; my salary was set at one hundred dollars per day, seven days a week. I could see that considerable perks would come with this unique position—hanging with Stan, shooting hoops and laughing till we peed our pants sounded pretty good to me. I have always loved the Beach Boys, so the idea that I was getting paid to help a favorite pop music legend get off drugs wasn't bad either.

On my third day on the job, I decided to take a Jacuzzi break in the patio area off the kitchen. I was soaking in the Jacuzzi when I noticed Brian walk into the kitchen and peer out onto the patio area. After peeking out three separate times, Brian walked out the back door wearing baggy shorts and a towel draped around his neck, headed straight for the Jacuzzi, and joined me.

"So, you and Stan were roommates in college?"

"Yeah, we were. We were best friends from the moment we met in summer school before our freshman year."

"So, you were a football player?"

"Sure was."

"I was a football player too," Brian smiled. "I was a quarterback in high school."

"Really? A quarterback, huh?" I said, surprised and impressed.

"Yeah, I could throw the ball pretty good. I was only second string, but I got to play some."

"Yeah, how did you like it?" I probed.

"Oh, man. It was scary at first, but I *did* complete my first pass."

"You completed your first pass—that's pretty good."

"Yeah! And I completed a touchdown pass on the last play of the season."

"No kidding," I exclaimed. "Hey, well, I had a hit record with the first song I ever wrote, 'Touchdown USA.'"

After a moment's hesitation, Brian let out a huge belly laugh, and I joined in. Stan came out and joined us in the Jacuzzi as Marilyn and her sister Diane watched in amazement from the kitchen window. They hadn't seen Brian so involved in a conversation, so animated—and laughing, no less—since recording hit single 45s back in the early Sixties, one hit after another.

When he was on fire with creativity, he routinely recorded hit songs on both sides of the 45s, in contrast to most groups, who'd just put a filler on the "B" side of their singles. Once he told me, "I could write a fart, and it would be a hit." He wasn't boasting, I came to learn. Brian was anything but egotistical.

That afternoon in the Jacuzzi, he locked eyes with me, and asked, "Do you ever hear voices?"

This off-the-wall question stunned me, and I hesitated and shot Stan a quizzical look before I answered.

"Uh, no, I can't say I have. Why—do *you*?"

"Oh, yeah!"

After a pause, I asked hesitantly, "So, what do the voices say to you?"

"Oh, man, you don't want to know. Really scary stuff."

Trying to put the conversation back on a more positive track, Stan jumped in and said, "Hey, Brian, look at it this way. This is your opportunity to quarterback the Beach Boys to another winning season. Whaddya say, big fella?"

Brian contemplated for a split second, then burst out, "You know what, you're right. Let's score some touchdowns—let's do it!"

Chapter Two

Last Ditch Effort

Let's back up a bit. This is a good time to explain some of the entangled Wilson and Love family history, introduce you to other assorted brothers and cousins, and give you some perspective as to why my best friend Stan and I entered the Beach Boys' orbit.

Stan had five family ties to the Beach Boys. Four were in the band: Stan's oldest brother, Mike Love, who has always been front man and lead singer, and his first cousins, Brian, Dennis, and Carl Wilson. Stan's middle brother, Stephen Love, was the Beach Boys' business manager.

The oldest Wilson brother, Brian is the gentle genius who co-founded what's often called America's Band in 1962. Enough about him for now; I'll fill you in on his challenges and accomplishments throughout *Beach Boys' Endless Wave*.

Brian's younger brothers, Dennis and Carl, are dead now. When they joined the Beach Boys in their middle teens, both boys had sweet voices and attitudes and did whatever their big brother and cousin asked of them. Dynamics sure changed as they grew up.

Mike Love, the oldest Beach Boy, has a long and involved relationship with his younger cousin, Brian. They co-founded the Beach Boys, and for years cooperated on songwriting. Mike has his own variety of hardworking genius; he's the invaluable mixture of glue and sweat that held the band together for decades.

Mike has always been the dependable Beach Boy, sober and present through thick and thin and thousands of gigs. As the frontman and lead singer, he embodied the Beach Boys image with his voice and mesmerizing stage presence. The Beach Boys would have folded in 1964 without him, and he's kept the band on the road for well over 50 years.

Even though he was not a family member, rhythm guitarist and vocalist Al Jardine was an important influence on the emergence of the band.

He was there when the group was still in high school, left for a while on the suggestion of his father to attend dental school, but luckily returned and stayed. Al sang the lead on the band's first number one hit song, "Help Me Rhonda."

His interest in folk music inspired Brian to arrange "Sloop John B" for the band to cover; and, Al later composed an unfinished original about his wife entitled, "Lady Lynda," which Brian helped him finish and the band recorded. It has been on their live stage play list ever since.

Stephen didn't aspire to be one of the Beach Boys; instead, he focused on academics and athletics. He was student body president of Morningside High School, class of 1965, and graduated seventh in his class of 535 students. Stephen was a star player on the Monarchs' football team and earned first team all-league honors as a wide receiver on offense and as a safety on defense. Playing both offense and defense is rare enough; winning first-team honors for playing both sides is almost unheard of.

Stephen was offered several football scholarships, including one to the University of Southern California, but he'd just had his heart broken by his high school sweetheart and he couldn't muster the requisite enthusiasm to play football at the college level. Instead, he decided to accept an academic scholarship at USC, thinking he should buckle down and learn something useful that would prepare him for a career.

Stephen excelled academically at USC, graduating magna cum laude with a Bachelor of Arts degree in Spanish in 1969. His grades were so good that he applied for and received a full-ride fellowship to USC's prestigious Graduate School of Business Administration.

The summer he graduated from college and before he started his two-year MBA program, Stephen visited his younger brother, Stan, in Eugene, Oregon. Stan played center on the University of Oregon basketball team, and he was fast becoming one of the top college players in the country.

As Stan's roommate and close friend, I met Stephen during his visit. Since I was a running back for the Fighting Ducks of the University of Oregon, our shared football background helped us become good friends. We just clicked. It takes courage, athleticism and intestinal fortitude to play the game of football, and we recognized and respected these qualities in each other. You could say we were cut from the same cloth.

Stephen began working for the Beach Boys full-time that summer, and he worked part-time in the group's office during the school year until he earned his MBA. He assisted the band's business manager, Nick Grillo, a man who was under a lot of pressure because the group was in decline, revenues were down, and the bills were piling up.

The band was not as popular as it had been before the

British Invasion. The music scene changed dramatically with the likes of the Beatles, Rolling Stones, Cream, and The Who. Jimi Hendrix had the bad taste to announce, "Well, we'll never have to listen to that lame surf music again," at the Monterey Pop festival in 1967.

That was, at best, mean-spirited crap in my opinion.

Since Brian had written most of the songs either alone or with Mike, he still received a good income from royalties, but the other Beach Boys' income mainly depended upon touring. They never managed to tone down their lavish lifestyles, and they were in dire need of cash. Brian and his wife Marilyn took it upon themselves to keep the group afloat during the band's lean days in the late Sixties and first few years of the Seventies.

Stephen's involvement in the business office was perfect timing. Even before he became manager, he brought fresh energy into a problematic scenario. The band (minus Brian) took to the road, and slowly but surely, a turnaround in their fortunes took place, as always, on the back of Mike Love, the reliable workhorse, day in and day out. In fact, if this book ever had an alternative title, it would be something like Mike Love—I'm Still Standing. (Kudos to the Rocket Man himself, Elton John, who is celebrating 50 years of music fame and fortune with a TV special titled—yup, you guessed it—"I'm Still Standing," after his enormous hit record of the same name.)

When Stephen took over the reins and replaced Nick Grillo as manager in April, 1972, momentum was finally building as the Beach Boys' concert tours became increasingly popular. One of Stephen's first major decisions was to start a repayment program from the band to Brian and Marilyn for $330,000 they'd poured into the group over the previous few years

Last Ditch Effort

(well over two million dollars in today's money). Stephen had Brian's back. When all the money was eventually repaid, Marilyn gratefully told Stephen, "Thanks for looking after us."

In 1972, the Beach Boys were commanding a pitiful baseline "performance fee" of only $5,000 per show. This was just the minimum fee for showing up—it didn't include a percentage of the gate or memorabilia sales, of course. During Stephen's tenure as manager, he ramped up the performance fee tenfold to $50,000 per show.

The first really big check the band got in the early Seventies was for a 1974 concert in Oakland, one that didn't include Brian. They sold out the stadium, and promoter Bill Graham

November, 1965, partying in the early days before fame, fortune, drugs and the excesses of the rock-and-roll lifestyle derailed Brian Wilson. This intimate party celebrated the release of a new album, Beach Boys Party! *Back row, left to right: Al and wife Lynda Jardine, Carl Wilson, Carol Botnick (friend of Marilyn Wilson), Dennis and his first wife Carole Wilson, Ron Swallow (roadie). Front row: Mike Love, in the company of adoring fans, Bruce Johnston (who toured as Brian's replacement), Brian with his wife Marilyn Wilson, and college freshman and future Beach Boys manager Steve Love.*

Photo by Stan Love
from the Larry Salisbury Collection

sent them a check for $150,000. Stephen took a picture of that check and framed it.

In 1975, Rolling Stone magazine recognized the Beach Boys as one of the biggest concert draws in the business, and they named the band's road crew, under the direction of workhorse Jason Raphalian, the best on tour. Stephen and the band were especially proud of that accolade.

However, touring and playing your greatest hits in every concert venue is one level of success; making creative new music is entirely another level. What was really going to put the Beach Boys back on top was Stephen's creative and risky "Brian's Back" campaign, a public relations masterstroke that led to the securing of a multi-million-dollar record deal with CBS Records in 1977. The new deal included a whopping $2 million cash advance against future album deliveries—worth well over $8 million in today's dollars. The deal's full potential was $8 million in 1977 dollars, or over $32 million today. It was one of the biggest music deals of the Seventies.

Under Stephen's guidance, the band would complete their deal with Reprise Records and join the CBS Records family.

The entire music industry was intrigued by the prospect of the long-idle Brian Wilson returning to active duty as a composer and producer. With the sold-out concert tours and new major label deal in place, the career of America's one-time favorite pop music group was undergoing a massive resurgence.

The viability of the CBS deal was contingent upon Brian Wilson's active participation: CBS insisted that Brian write and produce 75% of the new music. Though the Beach Boys were still viable on the road, they needed new music to feed the insatiable public beast or they'd fade from view.

If Stephen could get the musical wizard Brian Wilson to

compose again after a decade and record his matchless melodies and vocal arrangements, he might be able to orchestrate a complete resurgence of the band's career.

If Brian still had some magic left in his battered soul, he just might be able to recreate the lush sound he was so famous for, the harmonies that were a major component of the soundtrack of the Sixties. If the dormant genius could rise to the occasion and produce hit songs as he had before, doing his own version of Phil Spector's "Wall of Sound," the chances were good that their careers could be resurrected.

Brian cried when he signed the CBS contract. Could he miraculously create another hit record? For Brian, the thought was painful and frightening; he really wanted no part of fame or success again. After all, look what it had brought him before, nothing but heartache and disappointment. Brian had been a broken man for almost a decade.

Did he have the mettle to put his fragile self, his talent, and his soul on the line again? That was the multi-million-dollar question. We were going to see if Stephen could prop Brian up, with my help and Stan's, and get the golden goose to produce a hit record that would resonate with the times.

A lot had happened during the years that Brian had been in bed, not writing music, totally withdrawn from the band. Cocaine and heroin had become his drugs of choice. He would call his dealers at all hours, day or night, and tell them there was a thousand dollars in the mailbox (that always guaranteed a quick delivery). Brian was a physical and emotional wreck. At his peak weight, he carried over 300 pounds on his 6-foot, 3-inch frame, had greasy hair down past his shoulders, a scraggly beard, unclipped toenails, nicotine-stained fingers, and went unbathed for days, sometimes weeks at a time.

To further complicate the challenges he faced, Brian heard voices on a regular basis, voices sometimes telling him to harm people, or that people were about to harm him.

Brian had his first nervous breakdown two days before Christmas in 1964, when he suddenly left a concert tour, vowing never to tour again. Instead, he focused on writing new music for the band; he wanted to expand creatively and write with people of his own choosing.

Brian stayed home to write music over the next couple of years, and the Beach Boys toured without him. Brian's music evolved through several new albums in 1965 and 1966, with his masterpiece, Pet Sounds, coming out in 1966. In 1967, he was hard at work at what was to be its follow-up, Smile.

Mike was not happy with some of the esoteric lyrics Brian's new collaborators were writing. Though he recognized that Pet Sounds was a musical masterpiece, he knew what worked for the band. He thought Brian should stick to the proven and comfortable formula of surfing, hot rods and California girls, and he was essentially correct. It took years before Pet Sounds sophisticated brilliance was broadly accepted, and it never became a commercial hit.

Since the group's founding, Brian had always shared the credit with Mike because he was gentle, generous, and he'd looked up to his older cousin. In the early years, they shared the same vision of the band's sound and image—fun in the sun, bikinied babes, fast cars, and the California surf style of living.

Now all Brian wanted to do was stretch out and explore further reaches artistically, to compete with the likes of the Beatles.

In 1967, Mike's discomfort with Brian's new musical direction caused things to get more than a little heated. As portrayed in the film *Love and Mercy*, they had an ugly scene, and it brought things to a head. Brian had reached his breaking point; his mental and physical reserves were stretched so thin, he was done.

At that point, Brian effectively quit the band and withdrew into a cocoon of drugs and disenchantment. He vowed he would never write songs again for the Beach Boys, and he opted to slip into oblivion. He just couldn't take it anymore. He checked out. Why, he asked himself, should he continue shouldering the awesome responsibility that comes with writing the songs, doing the arrangements, teaching the others their parts, both vocally and instrumentally, slaving away in the studio, all the while dealing with a changing audience that was seemingly turning on him and his music?

Years went by and Brian stayed in his cocoon, sometimes not leaving his bedroom for months except to go downstairs to the kitchen and eat (and eat and eat). Brian had hit his lowest point. He was in the throes of addiction, a seemingly hopeless lost cause, and he'd been diagnosed as a paranoid schizophrenic. He had absolutely no interest in life, love, music or anything of value. Being a productive member of society was dead last on Brian's list of priorities. He was not interested at all in writing or recording new music, singing, or touring—those were the very things that had overwhelmed his childlike, overly generous, sensitive, and creative nature.

He was a defeated shell of a man, simply waiting to die. If ever there was a modern-day tragic Shakespearean character, Brian filled the role. He had, in the vernacular of surfers, wiped out.

Psychologist Eugene Landy was hired for the first time in 1975, but he was fired by Stephen after his fees climbed to over

$22,000 a month. Marilyn reached the end of her rope in 1976, when she felt Brian was a danger to himself and to the family. She threatened to have him committed to a mental institution.

Stephen pleaded with Marilyn to delay committing Brian and to give it one more try, take one last chance to save Brian. He asked her permission to hire his younger brother, Stan, to enter their home and drag Brian out of bed—against his will, if necessary—to try and save Brian's life. Marilyn acquiesced, thank God.

When Brian's youngest brother, Carl, learned about the arrangement, he enthusiastically said, "Smart move, Steve."

Mike was guardedly optimistic. His brother Stan was a professional basketball player who had a stint with the Lakers, but did that make him a qualified protector—essentially a life preserver?

Stephen lobbied hard. "Listen, Stan is our brother, he's Brian's cousin, and he's absolutely trustworthy. He has Brian's best interests at heart. That kind of loyalty isn't available anywhere else, at any price."

Mike agreed.

Stan's duties included making Brian take a daily shower, driving him to his psychiatrist, getting him to a gym for exercise, watching his diet, and eventually getting him back into the recording studio to write and record again for the first time in years. This was a monumental task, but Stan, who had come off a two-year stint with the Lakers, had the stamina and the discipline.

It wasn't smooth going at first. After years of not working and not getting out of bed, Brian had an aversion to doing anything except eating, sleeping, and taking drugs. He was rich and famous, used to making his own rules, and hellbent on

LAST DITCH EFFORT

fulfilling his subconscious death wish.

Brian steadily fought the idea of having a keeper, and he tried to fire Stan at the least provocation, ranting, "This is my house. Leave me alone! You're fired!"

Marilyn would always push back. "You either do what Stan tells you to do, or you're going to the mental hospital."

Clearly, Stan needed more backup in the extremely demanding, nearly impossible task of saving a lost soul who would go to any length to get drugs. That's when Stan suggested to Stephen that they bring me aboard to help.

This was the situation I walked into when Stan first brought me to Brian's mansion. I was hired the day after Stan introduced me to Brian and Marilyn, and Stephen's dynamic duo, as he referred to us, was in place. Stephen's No Drugs in Brian's Life policy was implemented with extreme urgency. "No drugs" wasn't just a policy, it was our law. No drugs of any kind, anytime, anywhere, from anybody. Ever, period!

Marilyn agreed; she wasn't a drug user and had never tried hard drugs herself—

Brian Wilson in the Sixties, smoking a little reefer before harder drugs grabbed him and wouldn't let go.

*Photo by Stan Love
from the Larry Salisbury Collection*

Brian (left) and Dennis Wilson. This is the perfect example of the Wilson brothers' contrasting styles and personalities—Dennis wildly leaping off the swing into space, Brian holding back in thoughtful puzzlement and wonder.

Photo by Stan Love
from the Larry Salisbury Collection

just wine, champagne, perhaps an occasional recreational puff or two of pot.

Stephen declared that if Stan and I couldn't keep drugs out of Brian's life, no one could. He said this with the resolute confidence of a born leader. He had sworn us to our task.

Our mission was to save Brian's life, a daunting undertaking, and we took it seriously. We monitored Brian around the clock. It wasn't easy. After all, Brian is a genius, and he would prove to be extremely crafty and resourceful when it came to feeding his drug habit. Brian didn't hesitate to approach complete strangers and beg them for drugs. Many were all too keen to accommodate him just because of who Brian is, a famous and legendary pop star. This was just one element of our ever-challenging task. Being vigilant 24/7 was the name of the game for our crew.

Stephen's last-ditch effort to avoid institutionalizing Brian worked, despite some surprising actions by Brian's own brothers, and despite every wily effort Brian made to get drugs. Brian did come back from the edge, and Stephen's Brian's Back campaign made the band richer than it had been in its heyday in the Sixties.

If a Hall of Fame for rock managers existed, Stephen likely would have been inducted. Instead, all too soon, he was exiled. I'll tell you the story, for I'm partly responsible for what happened; in my view, however, Stephen could be considered an unsung hero.

CHAPTER THREE

A Day in the Life

In the pre-Stan-and-Rocky days, Brian's coffee was a huge plastic mug, filled with five to six heaping tablespoons of instant coffee dissolved in scalding hot water, and chugged down in seconds. Brian paced back and forth until the caffeine kicked in, then he would lie down on a couch and pant. Yes, pant like a dog.

In those days, Brian asked the maid to fix him four eggs, sunny side up, with four strips of bacon and four links of sausage. He also downed four slices of white toast, slathered in butter and dunked in his eggs, and a mound of hash browns smothered in ketchup. He drank an enormous amount of milk with his morning meal, often just picking up the carton of milk and chugging a half quart at a time.

This was a surefire recipe for a heart attack waiting to happen.

We knew his routine had to change.

Once we had control, a typical day in the life of Brian Wilson began with a wake-up call from Stan and me, no later than 9:00 a.m. Then it was up and into the shower. Brian shaved with an electric shaver because his nervous system was too impaired to handle a razor with a sharp blade.

Being clean shaven with short hair was a new phenomenon for Brian. He'd had a beard and long hair for years, and suddenly one morning he took a pair of scissors, did a raggedy, half-ass job of cutting his beard and hair off, and came downstairs and lit a cigarette like nothing had changed.

"Brian, you look like a hobo," Marilyn laughed, and suggested Stan and I take him to a salon in Beverly Hills. After his eighty-dollar haircut and shave, we all agreed he looked damn handsome, and he decided to keep the clean-cut look.

His hair wasn't the only thing that was cut short. Serious coffee intake was bad for what was left of his frayed nerves, so we established a limit of two normal-size cups of brewed coffee in the morning.

Breakfast immediately became an 8-ounce glass of orange juice, freshly squeezed from the huge oranges that I picked from the trees in his backyard, a large bowl of health food cereal, two packets of Sweet'N Low, and a multi-vitamin.

Then it was off to the gym for an hour of basketball with Stan and me. We never had a problem getting a pickup game with the always-willing gym rats. Brian was an unorthodox player and he double-dribbled sometimes, but he loved to drive to the basket for a layup. Our opponents were thrilled to be on the court with Brian, and there was never a shortage of volunteers to play with him. Stan was a big draw, too; how many people get to play with an NBA player?

After our pick-up game, we sweaty three would take a quick shower, spend 15 to 20 minutes in a Jacuzzi, followed by a quick, cold shower. Then into the sauna for another 10 to 15 minutes of sweating, followed by yet another cold shower. After that, we took a ten-minute eucalyptus-scented steam bath, where Brian would cough his ass off until he eventually decreased his cigarette intake. Another quick cool-down shower followed, and then it was off to see the psychiatrist.

Brian had interviewed several psychiatrists before he found one he could relate to. Unfortunately, after nine months of Brian spilling his guts to his shrink, a guy he really liked, the doctor fell off a cliff while mountain climbing. His shrink's death was tragic, but it was doubly sad because it really affected Brian; it was the first time I'd seen him genuinely sad. Who knows what Brian revealed and how much progress was made? Now he had to start all over again with someone new.

Stephen gave me the background on Brian's past psychiatric care, including the lowdown on the infamous psychologist, Dr. Eugene Landy. Marilyn had hired him because of his reputation for successfully treating various celebrity types, plus he was amenable to making house calls.

Daily basketball was a big part of Brian's cure; it was the best part of the magical medicine Stan (left) and I (setting up the screen for Brian) put together to bring him back from his 311-pound self. Brian didn't take many shots against the 6'8" former LA Laker Stan, but he sure loved to dribble.
Photo by Stan Love
from the Larry Salisbury Collection

In fact, Landy preferred to provide his brand of psychotherapy in the home setting. In theory, it was his way of getting familiar

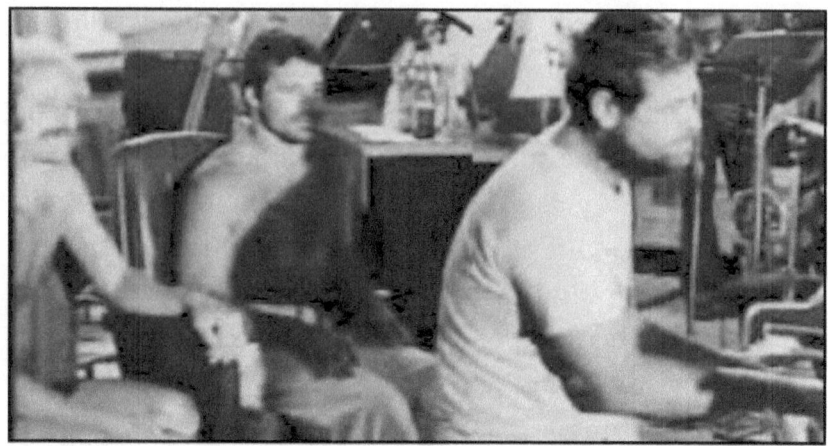

Stan and I had Brian's back, literally, wherever he was– on stage, at a piano on the road–it didn't matter. We were there!

Photo by and courtesy of Karen Love

with his patients, learning about their environment as well as the family dynamics. Stan thought it was a just a convenient way for him to save money on overhead expenses by eliminating the high cost of maintaining a pricey Beverly Hills office.

Marilyn agreed to Landy's fee of five thousand dollars a month for two weekly sessions with Brian, but within six months Landy increased sessions to three a week and upped his fees; he also billed travel time to and from his house. Landy stayed for two-hour sessions, and, at Marilyn's insistence, had meals or snacks. The two of them loved onion bagels with lox and cream cheese, topped with chives, red onion, and a squeeze of lemon.

Trouble started when Landy's fees continued to escalate monthly, finally hitting $22,000 per month after only six months.

Stephen had to step in and convince Marilyn that this was unheard of, both outrageous and unethical. Landy argued that his progress with Brian was well worth the expense. Stephen pointed out to the self-proclaimed "Guru to the Stars" that he had more than quadrupled his fees in less than six months.

After Marilyn gave Stephen permission to fire Landy, the doctor attempted a power play, insisting that his professional psychotherapeutic treatment was invaluable. This whole episode was explored in the movie, *Love and Mercy*.

It wasn't pretty, and it ended when Stephen personally informed Landy up close and in person that he could take his highly-self-rated professional services and seek employment elsewhere. Landy desperately tried to convince Marilyn that his services were worth every penny. Stephen escorted him to his car, and as he opened the car door for Landy, advised him, "If you ever retain another client at such exorbitant rates, the next time you might want to bring the bagels yourself."

Stephen set Brian up with a real psychiatrist the very next week, who got him on the proper doses of psychotropic medications for schizophrenia and bipolar disorder. They were key elements for stabilizing Brian.

The rest of the rehabilitation was on Stan and me: 24/7, day-in and day-out, week-after-week hypervigilance and preventing access to drugs. Stephen's edict was: No cocaine, no heroin, no barbiturates, no amphetamines, no marijuana, and no alcohol. (In the unenlightened Seventies, we didn't consider that the occasional dessert-like grasshopper qualified as real alcohol.)

That was the Stephen Love Law. Unfortunately for Brian's middle brother, it also translated to *No Dennis!* Stephen was explicit when he warned us that Dennis represented a serious threat to Brian.

Make no mistake, our task was by no means an easy matter; in fact, it was *extremely* challenging. Drug addicts can be exceptionally resourceful in the ways they go about acquiring drugs. The quest is phenomenally easier if they are also rich and famous. People everywhere and anywhere are only too happy to provide "party favors," by, say, slipping something to Brian just so they can claim that they partied with a Beach Boy.

These idiots convince themselves they are being cool, a good buddy, or a fast friend by sharing their pernicious poison with their idol. Instead, they seriously harm the recovering addict.

The job of Brian's protector is a painstaking one, and it never ends. Fending off setbacks is frustrating to anyone trying to save someone's life, or more to the point, saving someone from their self-destructive self.

But back to Brian's routine. After months of making inroads into solving Brian's major weight problem and making sure his mental health care needs were being met, Stephen, Stan and I made a concerted effort to get Brian to write songs.

Brian had three pianos in his house: the white baby grand in the sandbox at Brian's indoor beach, a black Steinway grand piano in the living room, and a quaint, upright piano in the parlor.

One day I was playing the upright when Brian's oldest daughter Carnie came in, jumped up on the bench next to me, and said, "My dad lets me sit here and he teaches me how to play." I knew that she had a lot of musical talent and Brian had been working with her.

I said, "Well, I don't think I can teach you how to play like your dad can, but you're welcome to play piano with me anytime."

Carnie surprised me by kissing my cheek, then she giggled and ran off. I sure wasn't surprised, though, when she, her sister Wendy, and their friend Chynna Phillips became famous musicians in their own right when they were barely out of their

A Day in the Life

A picture of an early Beach Boys Brain Trust– from left to right, Brian Wilson, with the Love brothers, Steve and Mike. Each played a role in building an endless wave.
Photo by Stan Love
from the Larry Salisbury Collection

teens. Their band, Wilson Phillips, sold ten million copies of their first album and had multiple number one hits.

Brian told Carnie and me that he sat on the piano bench between his father's legs when he was young and Murry taught him the basics of playing boogie-woogie. Brian didn't tell her, though, that when he took the rudimentary chord patterns and jazzed them up double-time, Murry couldn't keep up with his brilliant son. This is when Brian's musical genius blossomed and took off like a rocket. Murry marveled at Brian's innate talent, but not without feeling pangs of jealousy.

This is a good place to share an unsubstantiated story of how an enraged Murry picked up a plate one evening at the dinner table and smashed it into Brian's right ear. Brian had mentioned his father's gross habit of plucking out his glass eye and showing the boys his raw socket as punishment for their misdeeds, and Murry was furious that Brian brought it up at the dinner table.

Brian has never blamed his dad for having anything to do with his loss of hearing. Dennis Wilson was the source of many of the nasty rumors about the corporal punishment he and his brothers got. Dennis was also a habitual liar, and I can easily believe he exaggerated the severity of physical abuse meted out by Murry.

The abuse may be a rumor, but Brian's shattered eardrum is not. He's deaf in his right ear, and he's only heard "mono" sound for his entire songwriting and producing career.

When Stephen became the Beach Boys' manager, he knew he needed to better understand the Wilson boys' relationship with their dad. He visited his beloved aunt Audree, Murry's wife, and brought her a bouquet of flowers. Audree was best friends with Stephen's mom, Glee, Murry's sister, from the moment they met and sang together in a female trio at Washington High School in Los Angeles.

Stephen asked Audree outright, "Was Murry the ogre he has been made out to be in the press?"

She looked Stephen in the eye, shook her head, and said without hesitation, "No."

To my way of thinking, Audree gave the definitive and final word on that subject. Of course, she did love Murry and was protective of him, seeing him in a favorable light, even though it is a well-known fact that he could be an extremely rigid and harsh disciplinarian. It was also rumored he was a heavy drinker.

Back to Brian's state of mind at this point in his life: He had no interest in playing piano or any of the other many instruments he plays so well. In fact, Brian vehemently resisted playing music and, saddest of all, he refused to write songs.

Brian confided to Stan and me that for years he'd had no interest in creating any music. He described the process of

A Day in the Life

creating music as inducing a tidal wave of chaos and dissension that overwhelmed him. Brian said it had only brought him heartache, disillusionment, and disappointment. Stan and I repeatedly reassured Brian that that was in his *past* life. "This is your *new* life," we said, over and over.

We had a breakthrough when we convinced Stephen to book studio time at the band's recording studio in Santa Monica; we had hopes the old, familiar studio would rejuvenate Brian's interest in writing songs. With Brian being inactive for years, his brothers Carl and Dennis had taken over the studio. The two brothers formed a business partnership, Brothers Studio, so Brian's patronage was a welcome source of revenue for his younger brothers.

During Brian's first recording sessions, he would just pace around the room, scattered and distracted. In one early session, Stan was in the mixing booth, talking to the engineer, and Marilyn stopped by. As she and I talked in the hallway, Dennis suddenly appeared.

He jammed into the studio and tried to bum a cigarette and twenty bucks from Brian, who said, apologetically, "Marilyn never lets me carry any money."

Pissed off, Dennis split, slamming doors behind him. Though he didn't say another word to anybody, you could hear him swearing all the way down the hallway and out of the studio.

When we couldn't get Brian to write songs or even sit down at the piano, I suggested that Stan and I go into the soundproof recording room with Brian and sing (that's right, sing!). Brian burst out laughing whenever we sang songs that he liked, especially by the Righteous Brothers and Ray Charles.

Stan took friendly umbrage at Brian's derisive snorts. "Hey, Brian, I could laugh at you and the way you play basketball, ya know! We sing about as well as you dribble, cuz."

I added encouragingly, "But at least you're laughing, instead of just pacing around. Why don't you create something, Brian, so you won't have to listen to us sing?"

Brian thought this was so funny that he literally fell down laughing. When we got him back up on his feet, he sat down at the piano and played a sad, hauntingly beautiful melody. I guess our singing worked.

After he finished the song, I asked, "What's its name? Did you write it on the spot?" I hoped Brian would say that he had.

He answered enigmatically, "Shades of Blue and Purple Haunt Me."

"Is that the name of the song or just your reaction to our singing?"

Brian let loose with one of his famous belly laughs.

Though it didn't sound anything like a Beach Boy song, we pleaded with Brian to record it. He resisted until Stan said, "We'll let you have a grasshopper."

He couldn't sit down at the piano fast enough, and called to the engineer, "Let's lay one down . . . take one . . . a 1-2-3-4 . . ." and off he went, playing and singing. The engineer was barely able to roll tape in time. The song went something like:

It's over now, it's over now, shades of blue and purple haunt me.

Stan and I just stood there, speechless, when Brian finished. The engineer spoke up for the first time in a week. He said, "I guess that says it all."

Stan said, "I don't know what that means, or where that came from, but it's a start."

Brian laughed, "It's not a Beach Boys song," and he got up from the piano bench. An untrained observer might think that a first take would be mediocre and need improvement,

A Day in the Life

especially considering Brian's cigarette-ravaged voice, but Brian's performance was crystal clear and quite beautiful, almost angelic.

The engineer asked, "Do you want to do another take?"

Brian snapped his head around and said tersely, "No, it's fine." And it was—every note.

I whispered to Stan, "I guess when you've got the gift, it's easy."

Stan said, "That's one-take Brian for you."

As "It's Over Now," it was later re-recorded with Carl and Marilyn, though it wasn't released until many years later.

The next day Brian walked into the studio and started pacing, so I sang, "I'm going to sing until you're shades of blue and purple in the face. It's not over now. It's *not* over now. You still have so much music in you."

Brian slid onto the piano bench to stop me from singing my ridiculous lyrics and started playing and singing another song as sad and filled with longing as the renamed "Shades of Blue and Purple." The lyrics included:

"I know, I know, I know I'll find my love."

Later in the afternoon, he agreed to lay down a one-take track of that song, "Still I Dream of It." The next day, he did "Back Home," an older Beach Boy song, and he was on a roll, doing a track per day until he had done about a dozen songs.

Almost like he wasn't a part of the group, Brian said, "Now you guys can call the Beach Boys and tell them to come in and do their parts," which is exactly what we did. Other than Mike, the guys showed up about half the time, and *never* on time.

I'll never forget the first rehearsal I saw, watching Brian come alive and take over the room. When he talked, everyone shut up. He would start songs, then stop them suddenly and say things like, "Al, you're coming in late on the bridge and

I want you to play the first four bars very staccato," or, "Carl, you were flat on this note." The only person who never needed correction was Mike. He was always spot on.

Before Dennis got too drunk and wandered off, he would be allowed to lay down a drum track. The backup drummer, the always reliable Wrecking Crew-caliber Mike Kowalski, came in later to replace Dennis' amateurish clubbing technique on the final recording.

After one rehearsal, Mike took Stan and me next door to dinner, a place called Moonshadows. The vegetarian food wasn't half bad, but what I clearly remember is how I began to get a grasp on the dynamics of the ongoing Mike-Dennis battle. Mike was a sober guy, a meditator, and consistently reliable. Dennis most definitely was not. Mike had no tolerance for the drug bullshit Dennis pulled with Brian and his complicity in Brian's ten-year crash and burn.

Finally, dysfunctional or not, the Beach Boys finished *The Beach Boys Love You*, though it wasn't released until April of the following year.

Riding back home in the limo one day, I asked Brian how he wrote his songs.

"Writing songs is easy for me. I just let my subconscious take over."

Still curious, I asked, "So, tell me, Brian, do you ever let your conscious mind override your subconscious, so as *not* to produce a hit record?"

Brian darted his eyes at me, threw his head back, and let go with a resounding belly laugh.

The band told me a great story about the very early days of the Beach Boys when Brian's conscious mind produced a monstrous hit with the help of some subconscious inspiration.

A Day in the Life

When Brian heard Chuck Berry's hit single, "Sweet Little Sixteen," he knew the underlying music was a great starting point for the sound he'd been searching for. Mike and the rest of the band agreed.

Brian took that melody, wrote new lyrics and harmonies, and created the band's first major hit, "Surfing USA." The story gets a little strange for a minute

Chuck Berry, who was incarcerated at the time, maybe even for taking his own little "Sweet Little Sixteen" song a bit too much to heart, thought he'd been ripped off. As soon as he got out of jail, Berry took the Beach Boys to court for the infraction.

The band's attorney preempted the hearing at the last moment, literally in the courthouse hallway right outside the courtroom, by proving to Berry's lawyer's satisfaction that indeed, Chuck Berry had been properly credited for the music right on the record label. In fact, the record company had a big fat royalty check ready and waiting for him.

Mr. Berry ended up smiling, not scowling. The band was damn glad they'd done everything by the books. Chuck Berry sure wasn't a guy you wanted to cross.

A day in the life of Brian Wilson is always an enigma. You never know what you're gonna get.

And as if that weren't enough, much to everyone's surprise, Stan suddenly announced that he had a tryout with an Italian professional basketball team all lined up and would be flying to Rome very soon. As shocking as this news was to us all, Marilyn generously said she would buy Stan a first-class ticket so he could rest on his overnight flight and make a good first impression when he landed in Rome at 10 a.m. Marilyn was always very thoughtful that way.

When he arrived at Leonardo da Vinci International Airport, Stan was met by an eager coaching staff and was greeted warmly. After they exchanged pleasantries, the coaches said he had four hours before they expected him at a practice session that afternoon.

Stan stopped in his tracks, and said bluntly, "I need more time to rest. I can't possibly practice until tomorrow."

The coaches were shocked at his refusal. One said, ominously, "Be there today, or don't bother, Stan!"

Stan didn't bother. Without another word, he turned around and walked away from the coaches and back to the terminal, saying goodbye to his basketball career. That was it for him; he never played professionally again.

When I picked Stan up at LAX the next day, I had only one question. "I don't get it, man! You flew all the way to Italy; why didn't you at least go out there on the court and see if your jumper was working? Even the great Jerry West said you had a pure shooting stroke. I mean, you could have dazzled them. If it didn't work, *then* get back on a plane."

Stan said, tersely, "Fuck 'em!"

His decision was a damn lucky one for Brian, come to think of it.

Chapter Four

Owooooooo!

A few months into my new job of keeping Brian Wilson away from drugs and booze, I boarded a large private jet to join my first Beach Boys tour. The entire entourage waited wearily for the band's drummer and sex symbol to show up—the perennially late Dennis Wilson, Brian's younger brother. Dennis knew that the rest of the band would wait no more than thirty minutes before they left without him. The Beach Boys always had a back-up drummer on hand, just in case.

Dennis arrived in the nick of time, as I found he usually managed to do. He walked right past lead singer Mike Love and his brother Stan without saying a word. Dennis spotted me sitting next to Brian, about midway back in an aisle seat. I hardly knew Dennis, and I was momentarily awestruck by how handsome he was. He had a long, thick mane of sun-bleached hair, piercing blue eyes and a bold, confident swagger, as though he knew all eyes were on him—and they were. As were mine.

As he walked down the aisle, Dennis made a gesture with his outstretched arm, but it didn't quite register. He was coming closer with each step, and he seemed to be staring right at me.

The next instant, it was clear that he was flipping someone

Brian Wilson climbing the steps of a tour plane for the fist time in twelve years. The last time Brian was on a plane, in 1964, he'd suffered a nervous breakdown while on board and was hauled away by a psychiatric hospital intake van.

*Photo by Stan Love
from the Larry Salisbury Collection*

off. I looked around to see who it was, and I was stunned to realize he was flipping *me* off as he silently mouthed "Fuck you!"

Confused by his unexpected hostility, I was embarrassed and wondered what I had done wrong. The next moment, I was jolted back to reality. I knew, with absolute certainty, that I had to react to his blatant rudeness and disdain, or I would lose the respect of the entire Beach Boys crew and entourage before I really got to know them. I had to act. I *had* to confront Dennis and beat him at his own game—intimidation.

I jumped to my feet and opened my mouth. Damn, it was dry, and my voice cracked as I did my best to thunder, "What the *fuck* do you think you're doing, flipping me off? I'll stick that middle finger of yours up your ass, you little shit!"

Everyone shut up.

Owooooooo!

Dennis didn't say a word. He scurried by me, retreating to the rear of the plane where a barrel of Heineken was iced down for the roadies to enjoy. Dennis felt comfortable hanging with the road crew since those guys always fussed over him and told him he was the greatest. No one uttered a word about what had just happened.

The tour went off without a hitch, until the night Dennis showed up drunk and approached the center stage microphone to greet the fans. He made the bonehead mistake of yelling out, "Hellooooo, Toronto!"—but it was the day before we were scheduled to arrive in Canada. We were in Erie, Pennsylvania, a very different venue. His faux pas was met with boos and he realized his error, but he was too drunk to remember what city he was in. He tried to apologize to the audience by slurring, "It's been a [hiccup] long trip."

An aggravated fan yelled, "Don't trip and fall on your drunk ass!"

Dennis flipped off the fan and shouted, "You're lucky I don't come out there and trip *your* ass—I mean, *kick* your ass."

Level-headed Carl Wilson managed to convince Dennis to retreat to his drums, but as he staggered back, he tripped and fell into the high-hat cymbal, knocking it over. There was a loud *crash-boom-bang*.

As Dennis crawled onto his stool, Carl tried to cover for him, "Don't mind Dennis. He went surfing today and his board hit him in the head."

A wag in the audience didn't buy Carl's feeble explanation and yelled, "Where did he go surfing, in a bathtub full of booze?" Laughter erupted, plus a din of boos.

Dennis fumed, and he began to shout obscenities at the crowd. When he suddenly fell backwards off his stool, he got a rip-roaring round of applause. Another witty fan shouted, "Ride that wave, Dennis. Surf's up!"

Brian surprised everyone when he stepped forward, and in a commanding voice he counted down *1-2 . . . and 1-2-3* and the concert got underway. Brian modified the usual set list and began the concert with "Surfer Girl" since that song doesn't require drums to make it work. The change gave the roadies time to reconfigure the drums for the backup drummer, Mike Kowalski, who jumped in as Dennis staggered off, swearing to himself and flailing his arms and fists in the air à lá Don Quixote. Brian's quick thinking undoubtedly saved the show.

The band traveled to Toronto the next day. Stan and I took Brian for a walk on a trendy street near our hotel. Several people noticed Brian, said their hellos and asked for autographs. Brian happily obliged. Some called out, "We love you, Brian!" Brian persuaded us to stop in a jazz bar because, he said, the band playing sounded "really great."

This was a ruse. What Brian *really* wanted was a grasshopper, his favorite cocktail. We sometimes let him have one as a treat; there wasn't much alcohol in the drink (it is equal parts crème de menthe, crème de cacao, and cream, and is pretty much an after-dinner chocolate mint). No sooner had we grabbed seats at the bar than Brian pleaded with us to let him have one, saying that he deserved a reward for having bailed out the show with "Surfer Girl."

The guy sitting next to Brian said, "Yeah, let him have one. I'm buying."

The bartender and others within earshot looked at us, waiting to see what would happen next. Not wanting to look like an asshole, Stan said agreeably, "Yeah, sure. Why not? Brian did a great show last night, but we have another show to do tonight,

Owoooooo!

so just one, barkeep." The bartender made a big pour. Stan and I looked at each other apprehensively and ordered beer.

Brian chugged his drink down in nothing flat and eyed the blender. "Can I have what's left?" The bartender refilled Brian's glass without even giving us a look. Brian chugged that one down too, and then sat there squinting, his eyes shut tight from the sting of the brain freeze.

A few seconds later, the guy seated next to Brian noticed the grimace on his face and asked, "Are you all right?"

Brian, without opening his eyes, shook his head and said, "Can you get me another one?"

Stan interceded, "Not right now, Brian. You've got a show to do tonight."

The friendly guy said, "Well, it's nice to meet you, Brian. My name's Ralph." The moment Ralph reached over to shake Brian's hand, Brian threw up all over the guy's shoes. It happened so fast and was so unexpected, the guy didn't have a chance to dodge the stream of green, frothy vomit, but he did manage to say, with a smile, "Well, I've been called Ralph my whole life, but I've never been ralphed on before."

Stan apologized to Ralph as I asked the bartender for a rag soaked in club soda and wiped off the guy's shoes. Brian just sat there in a daze. Ralph was a real sport. He said, "I never liked these shoes anyway. Besides, now I can tell my friends a Beach Boy ralphed on me." We got Brian out of there after we bought Ralph another beer and picked up his tab.

When we got back to the hotel, we only had about an hour before we needed to leave for the stadium for that night's concert. Brian plopped down on the king-sized bed in the bedroom and took a power nap. Stan stretched out on the living room sofa, thumbed through the hotel tourist guide magazine, and snacked on the complimentary fruit basket. I called Marilyn to give her a quick update without mentioning anything about Ralph (or ralphing).

As it turned out, Brian's puking was just the beginning of a very strange evening. It must have been the grasshoppers; I've never been able to come up with a viable reason for his actions.

The three of us walked out of the hotel when a parade was going by right in front of the lobby, with a colorfully dressed clown juggling three red balls in the air, the same size and color as his nose, bopping up and down as he danced along. Out of the blue, Brian bolted right into the thick of things, and he started flailing away at the unsuspecting clown.

Caught completely off guard, Stan and I were a beat behind, and it took us a second or two to react and push our way into the crowd to grab Brian. We pulled him off the poor clown, who was frantically covering up his head to fend off Brian's flurry of punches. The attack was startling and shocking because Brian has always been absolutely nonviolent. He's never been in a fist fight in his life.

Stan barked, "What the hell was that?"

"I thought it was someone I know," Brian mumbled.

"Someone you *know*? You thought that clown was someone bad?"

"Yeah, he looked like someone who did me wrong."

The three of us had to go around the corner to avoid the rest of the parade and get to our limo. Stan and I were shocked by Brian's hostility. We had an unusually introspective, contemplative ride, and Brian appeared to settle down by the time we got to the venue. We left the limo, entered the roped-off backstage talent area, and started walking toward the hospitality section. The other Beach Boys were scattered about, schmoozing with

Owooooooo!

various VIPs, "holding court," as they say in show business.

Stephen stepped up to greet Brian with a handshake, and Brian uncharacteristically hugged him. Everyone noticed this unusual show of affection.

Brian suddenly broke off the hug and bolted for the second time that evening, this

Brian Wilson, clean and sober but still in recovery. Stan Love and I kept him close and under 24/7 supervision. Brian could still be paranoid and strange, always an enigma.

*Photo by Stan Love
from the Larry Salisbury Collection*

time charging straight towards his cousin Mike, who was standing quietly with his back against a wall. Horrified, I watched Brian launch a ferocious surfer-stomp kick at Mike's groin. With great reflexes, Mike rolled sideways and avoided a direct hit in the balls, though he clearly absorbed quite a blow.

Stan grabbed Brian before he could get off another kick.

Completely shocked, I put my arm around Brian and gently turned him around. I said quietly, "*Easy*, big fella. What's going on, Brian? Talk to me."

"I'm cool now." Brian kept his back turned on Mike, who looked hurt and embarrassed as hell, and began an unrelated but animated conversation with Stephen about, of all things, surfing.

"So, you really like to surf?"

"Brian, I love to surf."

"Can I go with you sometime? I'll probably fall on my ass, but so what? We'll have fun!"

Stephen laughed, "Everyone falls on their ass, that's part of the fun. You wipe out and you get back up again. Just like in life."

Brian said earnestly, "Yeah, that's right. But do you think I can learn to surf?"

"Brian, you were a football player. I have no doubt you can become a surfer."

By now, Stephen and I felt we had the situation with Brian under control. Stan went over to console Mike, who was traumatized and shocked by his nonviolent cousin's attack in front of dozens of stunned onlookers. Everyone was wondering what the hell Mike did to provoke this onslaught of hostility from our Brian, the mild, ever-peaceful gentle spirit.

Despite the bizarre preliminaries, the big Toronto show went fine that night and came off without further incident. In fact, I had never seen Brian more relaxed during a performance.

Mike, on the other hand, was distracted, to say the least. When your bandmate/cousin attacks a clown and then attacks you for no discernable reason, all bets are off. Mike wanted this show over, now. He avoided his normal spot where he usually stood to avoid Dennis' lethal drumsticks, left of center stage next to Brian, and he stuck to center stage right in front of the drums.

Dennis had an unorthodox drumming style—he held the thin end of the sticks and hit the drum with the thick end for maximum volume. His reverse technique led to an extraordinary number of broken sticks as well as extra noise, and when they broke, they flew onto the stage and hit whoever was in front of him.

Grinning, Dennis quickly broke two drumsticks that shot straight out at Mike. During the rest of the performance, Mike

Owooooooo!

darted around and looked over his shoulder like he couldn't wait to get off the stage.

Dennis was reveling in Mike's discomfort. Just before intermission, Dennis left his drums and went to the center stage microphone and announced, "I love you, Brian!" Then he sang an *a cappella* version of "You Are So Beautiful," a Joe Cocker song that went over especially well since Dennis' cracked voice resembled Joe's raspy tones.

A few days later, we returned to southern California and Brian's beloved Bel Air haven. He entered his mansion cheerfully, bellowing the lyrics to "Home Sweet Home," which took Marilyn, by surprise. Laughing, she asked Stan and me, "What's that all about?"

Stan let me field that question. "Why don't you fill her in?"

Brian howled like a wolf, "Owooooooooo!"

Marilyn gave me a wide smile. "Will you please fill me in, Rocky?"

I smiled back. "Here, Marilyn, I want you to sit down and make yourself comfortable while I pour us a glass of champagne. You're gonna need it." I opened a chilled bottled of Dom Perignon from the office bar and carefully poured two Baccarat flutes to the very top.

Grinning, Stan and Brian sat down next to Marilyn, and I remained standing as I gave her a blow-by-blow reenactment of Brian's first tour in a decade, starting with Dennis falling into the drums and Brian saving the day with his quick-thinking impromptu countdown of "Surfer Girl" to start the show.

To my surprise, we made it through the grasshopper debacle with Brian ralphing on Ralph's shoes without a word from Marilyn; she was wide-eyed and shaking her head in disbelief at the idea of Brian pouncing on the unsuspecting clown dancing by in the parade. Her jaw dropped when I graphically described Brian surfer stomping Mike.

Marilyn looked at her mild-mannered husband, calmly sitting there as though I was talking about someone else. "Brian, what on earth got into you?"

Brian just looked at her, shrugged, and gave her a goofy smile. He looked like a ten-year-old boy who was trying to wiggle out of trouble.

Marilyn shook her head at her usually nonviolent husband. "This doesn't mean you're turning into a brawler now, does it, Brian?"

"No."

"Well," Marilyn said, "I really don't know what to make of all this, but I do think we need to celebrate your getting back on the road and coming home safely. Where do you want to go, Brian?"

"Where else?" Brian sang out, "The Luau!"

Beating Brian to the punch, Stan interjected, "And yes, Brian, you can have one grasshopper."

Brian started dancing around, singing and howling, "Owoooooo! Who's that I see hiding in these woods? Owoooooo! You're everything a big bad wolf could want! Listen to me, I don't think you should go walking in these spooky old woods alone. Owoooooo! Let's go to the Luauuuuuu, the place that drive us wolves mad. Just to see that you stay safe, I think I oughta walk with you for aways. Owoooooo!"

Marilyn, Stan, and I were all chiming in with Owoooooos of our own when the doorbell rang. The door opened, and as Stephen walked in, he was greeted by a chorus of wolf howls.

Laughing, Stephen asked, "What's going on?"

"We're celebrating getting home safely," Stan yelled.

Owooooo!

I handed Stephen a flute of Dom Perignon.

Marilyn hugged Stephen and said, "We're going to the Luau. You're coming with us."

Brian put his arm around Stephen and said, "Thanks for hiring Stan and Rocky!" He followed with an exuberant "Owoooooo!"

Marilyn said, "I'm gonna call a limo. We're all partying tonight. Are you up for it, Steve?"

Stephen and Brian grinned, and we all howled, "Owoooooo!"

We never did figure out what had triggered Brian's behavior that night. He sure can be mysterious sometimes.

Chapter Five

The Troubadour

Early in 1977, Marilyn answered a call from Danny Hutton of Three Dog Night. Danny was one of Brian's old party buddies, and one of his favorite singers. Brian often said about Danny, "He has some pipes."

Danny was also a babe magnet. He and Brian had been notorious for carousing and hell-raising together, these two rich, famous musicians, boozers, and drug gluttons. *Nothing* was off limits. They had no boundaries, and when it came to drugs and excess, those two wrote the book. Rumors had it that they'd take two or three hits of acid when everyone around them was taking one. But then, who's counting?

Danny and Brian's idea of a weekend spree wasn't a couple grams of blow, it was a couple of eight balls (an eighth of an *ounce* of coke each). And when they took delivery, they'd ask the dealer, "Can you get us more if we need it? You never know who we're going to run into. Here's an extra hundred. Stay by the phone."

When Danny called, he swore to Marilyn that he was off drugs. He must have been convincing, because Marilyn decided to make an exception this once and allow Brian to hang with him that Saturday night. Still, I know one of the main reasons for her letting him off the short leash was her belief that Stan and I could handle the situation.

After all, Brian was finally touring again after more than a decade.

Marilyn was just beginning to give Brian some freedom, and she had started to encourage him to venture away from his beloved Bel Air estate, his all-too-safe haven. The three of us didn't want Brian to settle into agoraphobia. He had to start coping in public—another reason for her agreeing to the night out.

Brian needed to function well in public pretty soon, because he'd agreed to take Marilyn to Saint-Tropez, their first vacation in five years. Marilyn had been dying to go to the Riviera hot spot for ages—it was a mecca for the jet set, the "in" spot for the rich and famous. She had already made reservations at the Byblos Hotel, the ultra-cool place to stay.

On our big night out with Danny Hutton, Stan and I drove Brian to the Cock 'n Bull restaurant on Sunset Boulevard and Doheny Road. We arrived at 7:00 and joined Danny at his table. Danny was already three sheets to the wind, mindlessly pushing his food around on his plate, and singing something in a Brian-like falsetto.

After watching fifteen minutes of incoherent non-interaction between Brian and Danny, Stan looked at me, rolled his eyes, and asked, "Hey, you guys, want to go to the Troubadour?"

"Yeah!" was the immediate and unanimous response.

Danny left a hundred-dollar bill on the table and off we went, but not before he slipped and fell getting into Brian's limo. Danny turned to our sober Brian, and laughed, "It's not a party until *somebody* falls down!"

We arrived at the Troubadour, a famous West Hollywood

nightclub, and turned the limo over to the valet. The owner, Doug Weston, greeted us warmly, and said, "Well, well, well, what do you know? First Bob Dylan and Joan Baez, and now Brian Wilson and Danny Hutton. What a star-studded night!" He comped all four of us.

Brian said, "I want to sit with Bob."

Stan gave me the task of asking the famously reclusive Dylan if we could join him. I nervously approached the living legend, and politely said, "Excuse me, I'm Rocky Pamplin, and I work for Brian Wilson as one of his personal staff. He and Danny Hutton would like to know if the four of us could join you and Joan."

Dylan looked at me apprehensively, turned and conferred with Joan, who whispered something to Bob, who looked back at me, halfway smiled, and asked, "Where's Brian?" Brian was pacing nervously nearby; he stopped and stared at a wall, showing his unmistakable profile. Bob checked him out, and more enthusiastically said, "Sure!"

The four of us made our way to Bob's table. Brian sat down next to Dylan and asked, "You got a cigarette?"

Dylan nodded, and Brian took one.

"Got a light?" Brian asked next.

Dylan agreeably picked up his lighter and lit Brian's cigarette. Brian didn't say a word; he hot-boxed the cigarette until it was almost down to the filter.

Dylan said, "You look good, Brian. You lost a lot of weight, didn't you?"

"Yeah, I lost a hundred pounds. My wife put locks on the refrigerator doors, and Stan and Rocky and I play basketball every morning."

"Sounds like that plan is working well for you."

Brian grinned, "Yeah, we're undefeated!"

"That's great. I'm happy for you." Dylan reached out, touched Brian's arm, and added earnestly, "Congratulations!"

Brian, feeling a little overwhelmed, leaned back in his seat and met Bob's kind, intense gaze. A few seconds went by, and Brian's eyes suddenly filled and began to overflow. The table was awkwardly silent.

Brian stubbed his cigarette in the ashtray, and blurted, "I gotta go."

He got up and charged off, and I leaped to my feet and followed. We were a few feet away when I whispered, "Brian, why don't you say goodbye to Joan and Bob."

Brian half turned, muttered a quick "Bye," and kept walking.

Before I caught up with him, I turned back to the table, looked at Bob and Joan, shrugged, and said with a perplexed look on my face, "Rock stars. Hmm . . . ."

Bob and Joan chuckled.

Later Stan told me that Danny got up, shook Bob's hand, and said apologetically, "You know Brian."

A mystified Dylan, disappointment in his voice, said, "No, not really. I've never met him before. I feel like I still haven't. But he looks great, he looks real clean."

Stan introduced himself then. "Bob, sorry about that. I'm Brian's cousin; Mike Love's my brother, and my other brother, Stephen, manages the Beach Boys. He hired my friend Rocky and me to help rehabilitate Brian."

Dylan said, "Sounds good. Looks like that's going pretty well, too."

"So far so good," Stan agreed, and left.

When Danny and Stan caught up with us, Brian said he wanted to go upstairs to the VIP room. Doug Weston said, "No problem," then he whispered to Stan and me, "Do you think he'll stay longer up there than he did at Dylan's table?"

Stan shook his head, "I doubt it."

Upstairs, people recognized Brian as soon as he walked into the room. They scrambled to offer him drinks, and some slicksters tried to slip him drugs. Stan and I were on full alert, and we confiscated and returned it all.

Stan announced loudly to everyone in the room, "Brian's turning over a new leaf. *Please*, don't give him any drugs—okay?"

Danny had an announcement of his own. "Drinks are on me. I'm buying a round for the house."

Everyone cheered. Danny looked at Brian, and then at Stan, who nodded and said curtly, "*One* grasshopper—no vodka. And don't even think about trying to slip something in it, Danny."

Brian chugged his drink and plopped down in the nearest chair, looking slightly uncomfortable and thoroughly bored. I wasn't surprised, when, five minutes later, he said, "Let's go." As Brian bolted for the door, Stan quietly reminded him to say goodbye. Without looking over his shoulder or missing a step, Brian said curtly, "Later, Danny."

Hutton said plaintively, "But the party just got started, Brian."

Brian couldn't get out of there fast enough.

That was his big night out on the town.

Stan drove, and I sat in the back of the limo with Brian. I turned to Brian, the eccentric musical genius, and asked seriously, "Did you have fun tonight, Brian?"

He looked at me. Without answering the question, he said with a sigh, "I guess we have to go out on that big international tour this year."

Feeling exasperated, I sighed back at Brian with a theatrical flair, and said, dripping with sarcasm, "Man, you're too much. I wish *my* biggest problem in life was having to go on tour and perform in front of adoring fans who scream, 'We love you, Brian!' I mean, what a bummer, performing in front of tens of thousands of cheering fans. There's all that applause and adulation you have to contend with. Singing is such sad, sorrowful business. You poor thing."

Brian was his sweet, docile self during my sarcastic harangue, staring out of the window to his right. Suddenly he shifted his stare to his left, hardly moving his head. He met my eyes.

And without warning, he threw his head back and cut loose with a rip-roaring belly laugh—one of the deep-down, honest guffaws he's famous for.

Chapter Six

It Must Be the Squab

Before we left for our St. Tropez vacation, Stephen told us he heard rumblings of dissent within the ranks of the Beach Boys. We thought it was ridiculous, because he'd just signed the Beach Boys to CBS Records for a record-breaking $8 million contract (which included a $2 million cash advance) and set up a tremendous 40-city European tour.

Stephen thought it would be a good idea to meet with Marilyn, Brian, Stan, and me before our 10 p.m. flight to Paris. Marilyn made a reservation at Mr. Chow's in Beverly Hills so the five of us could have a nice pre-vacation tête à tête and discuss the latest band politics. We agreed it was a good excuse to get together and do what rich and famous people do to pass the time—eat, drink, and hang out.

We got a great window table between Jack Nicholson and his beautiful lunch companion Diane, and John Derek and his gorgeous, *very* young wife Bo on the other side. The four of them were well acquainted, and they were chatting away when our less-famous party of five was seated in the middle. Menus were proffered and drink orders taken; we ordered a nice bottle of Pouilly-Fuissé.

Jack looked at Stan, quizzically, "You look familiar. Were you on the Lakers?"

"Yeah, my name is Stan Love." He reached out to shake Jack's hand. "It's good to meet you. Say hi to my cousin Brian Wilson and his wife Marilyn." He pointed, "And that's my brother Stephen, manager of the Beach Boys, and my friend Rocky."

Everyone nodded. Stan continued, "You actually cast Rocky in the movie you directed at the University of Oregon, *Drive, He Said*."

Jack was confused. "Really? Which part?"

I said, "That would be the unforgettable role of the M.P. But I didn't get to play the part. I promised my sister I would take her to her senior ball at Chico State. But I did attend the wrap party. You threw up on my shoes."

Brian jumped in, "I'm usually the one who does that."

Everyone laughed.

"Ah, yes, the wrap party. *Now* I remember," Jack smiled.

"I still have those shoes. Never cleaned them. I kept them as sort of a memento. I didn't get to play the M.P., but I brag about getting barf on my shoes—from Jack."

As we laughed, Marilyn chuckled and wrinkled her nose. "I think I just lost my appetite."

The waiter appeared with the wine, opened and served it with a flourish, and took our orders. Stan said to Jack, "I liked *Drive, He Said*, even if you didn't cast *me* in it."

"Well, that makes ten people who liked it," Jack grinned, good-naturedly.

I laughed. "Well, besides throwing up on my shoes, you did throw one *hell* of a wrap party."

There was laughter, and John Derek said, "If it's any consolation, Jack, I also saw *Drive, He Said*, and *I* liked it, too.

It Must Be the Squab

Jack laughed, "One more, and we've got an even dozen people who liked it. Let's just say it was my first and last directorial effort. I leave that part of the business to the professionals now."

John Derek turned to me and asked, "Are you an actor?"

Stan Love (left) with my sister Sandra and me. While out to dinner one night with Brian Wilson and others, Sandy became a topic of conversation when I told Jack Nicholson her prom kept me from playing a role in his directorial debut movie, Drive, He Said.
Photo by and courtesy of Sandra Ficalora

I answered, "Let's just say I'm a 'studying actor.' I prefer that to 'struggling actor.'"

"The reason I ask," John continued, "Bo and I are in the preliminary stages of planning some movies, including one a few years down the road called *Tarzan and Jane*. I'm sure there's a part in there that you might be right for . . ."

I barged in, "*Which* part?"

Everyone laughed, and Jack said, "Sounds like you might be able to do comedy."

"Well, right now my acting coach has me working on walking, talking, and chewing gum at the same time. I do get a lot of laughs."

The waiter reappeared and served the appetizers, including the house specialty, squab. Brian asked, "What's that?"

Marilyn explained. "Well, Brian, it's baby pigeon on a bed of arugula."

"Arugula? Baby *what*?"

Marilyn assured him, "It's delicious, Brian. Just try it."

Brian popped a piece in his mouth. "Boy, that's good. Where'd you learn about this?"

Marilyn was not amused. "Well, Brian, *I've* been living a life while *you've* been in bed the last ten years."

The tables got a little quiet. Brian didn't respond to the barb. He called, "Hey, waiter, can we get more squab?"

Stan warned, "Brian, remember you're on a diet."

Brian was resigned. "How can I forget? Talk about lifesavers, literally."

"Gotta watch your cholesterol, Mr. Rock Star," Stan said.

It was fun; all three tables were relaxed, sharing small talk. Jack and Stan were talking basketball, Marilyn, Diane, and Bo were chatting away, and John engaged Brian in a conversation about his music and the good old days.

Best of all, Brian was enjoying himself. He and John were laughing and carrying on. Stephen and I focused on enjoying the delicious squab.

We were finishing up the appetizers a few minutes later, when John Derek turned to me. "So, Rocky, is that your real name?"

"No, it's Rushton, but I never felt like a Rushton."

"Rushton, huh? That's unusual. I like it. Have you been in anything lately?"

"Nothing big. A couple of bit parts and a few commercials."

Marilyn broke in, "He's the new Winston Man. He's on all the billboards nationwide."

Bo said, "That's where we've seen you."

Jack's date Diane said, "Oh yeah, you're the one with the open shirt at the beach."

It Must Be the Squab

Stan laughed, "I told you they don't even look at your face,"

Bo and Diane said, in unison, "Oh, yeah, we do!"

John said, "I actually pointed to your billboard once and said to Bo, why isn't this guy a leading man? You should be—unless you can't act. Well, Rushton, so *can* you walk, talk, and chew gum at the same time—without knocking over the furniture, that is?" (This was an old actor's joke.)

"Yes, as long as the lights are on... but then I still have trouble with the talking part. I *do* have the chewing gum part down."

Diane laughed and said, "He's funny."

I asked, "Now, John, on this Tarzan movie, will there be furniture in the jungle?"

I popped the last morsel of squab into my mouth just as Brian asked, "Can you pass the squab, Rocky?"

I swallowed. "Oops."

John handed me a card. "Bo has some stuff in the pipeline now, but please stay in touch, Rocky."

"Thank you, John, I certainly will."

John and Bo said they had to go and excused themselves. John said, "It was nice chatting with everyone, and, Brian, it's great to see you back in action. Please give us more of your wonderful music. You are truly an American treasure."

Brian said, shyly, "Ok."

John looked at Jack and said, "As always, it's been nice. I'll have my girl call your girl next week about a tee time."

Air kisses and *ciaos* were exchanged all around. As Jack and Diane left a few minutes later, Jack said, "Nice to see all of you. And Brian, let me just say, I, too, am a fan. So please give us more of your good vibrations."

"I will, Jack. And by the way, I flew over the cuckoo's nest, too!"

There was a ripple of laughter from the eavesdroppers.

As the entrées were being served, Stephen said, "Well, that was entertaining. Quite the luncheon spot you have here, Marilyn."

"Ah, there's nothing to it when you're married to an American treasure."

Stan added, "Yeah, Brian, ya see? Everybody loves you. Isn't that what I've been telling you?"

I reinforced Stan's message. "The whole world loves you, Brian."

Stephen picked up his wine glass and said, "I'll drink to that! Here, here, Brian!" We clinked glasses. Brian ignored us and focused on devouring his filet mignon.

"And just think, Rocky might wind up being Tarzan," Marilyn said breathlessly.

"I thought he was going to play Jane," Stan teased. There was another smattering of laughter from a few patrons within earshot.

I went along with the joke. "Hey, I'll play the chimpanzee, as long as they spell my name correctly in the credits!"

Stan said, with an evil grin, "At least you'll be wearing a loincloth to play Tarzan, Mr. Centerfold."

I laughed and said, half-seriously, "I don't want to be known for my body; I want to be known for my mind."

"You might be in the wrong town for that," Stephen laughed.

Brian asked, "Do we *have* to go on vacation to St. Tropez tonight?"

"Yes, Brian," Marilyn answered quickly. "I know it's a tough job, but someone's got to do it. We haven't been on a vacation in like forever. Besides, I bought two new bathing suits and all-new Cartier luggage."

It Must Be the Squab

"Do they have squab there?" Brian asked.

Before Brian could get his important question answered, the waiter approached to clear the plates and asked, "Would anyone like dessert?"

Brian quickly asked, "Can we have some more squab?"

Marilyn answered for the group. "No, no more squab and no desserts. We're all on diets, at least Brian and I are." Turning to her husband, she said, "See the sacrifices I make for you, Brian? Besides, we're going to be on a world-famous beach for a week and I've got to fit into my new bathing suits."

"Oh—me too," Stan joked.

I teased, "Will your bathing suit be a one piece or a two-piece bathing suit, Stan?"

"At least I won't be naked!" Stan shot back.

Brian got a worried look on his face. "You're not going to be naked, are you, Rocky?"

"No, but a lot of the French chicks will be topless."

That clinched it for Brian, and his face showed it. "Okay, I'll go!"

"Oy vey," Marilyn said. Then she turned her attention to the business manager and asked, "So, Stephen, what's the latest?"

"Well," Stephen began slowly, "We've been having so much fun that I hate to spoil our good time with the latest from Carl, Mike, and Dennis. In my book, things are going well—the CBS agreement, the big European tour, the excellent new album coming out. In theirs, they're not happy with anything I'm doing. There's a lot going on under the surface—those three are generating trouble."

Marilyn said seriously, "Stephen, I'm not worried. You're a hero in *my* book for not caving in to them like everyone else does. It's called integrity, and you have it, Stephen. You're the only manager the Beach Boys ever had that *has* had it."

Stephen, Stan, and I grinned. This was Marilyn at her coolest.

"What this is *really* about," Stephen explained, "is just that Mike's pissed at me. I sent him a telegram while he was in Switzerland at that six-month meditation retreat and reminded him that the Beach Boys have a major European concert tour kicking off in Leningrad in just a couple of months. I reminded him in no uncertain terms that this is the first time any American band will perform in Russia—it's groundbreaking, it's monumental, it's historic. And then I imprudently said, 'Now is not the time in your life to be stupid.' That wasn't the best choice of words on my part. I also told him he needed to get his ass back to the States for rehearsals."

Little did we know at the time that Stephen's telegraphed rebuke would create a rift between talent and management, one that'd create enormous repercussions. While he was the manager, Stephen was still an employee—he worked for Mike and the rest of the talent. It's a rift as old as the hills in the entertainment business. Walking onstage and commanding the attention of thousands of fans strokes an ego that managers must handle damn carefully. Once the talent becomes seriously offended, as Mike had been, the balance of power is forever skewed.

When you factor in Mike's role in hiring Stephen in the first place, then pepper that with some sibling rivalry (a younger sibling, at that), the road to forgiveness is a long, rocky one.

Brian seemed surprised. "I didn't know that Mike's mad at Stephen."

Stan added, "Mike has thanked me at least half a dozen times for bringing Rocky onboard. Every time the subject comes up, I remind him that it was Stephen's idea to not only hire Rocky, but first to hire *me* to bring 'Brian Back.'

"Brian wouldn't have lost a hundred pounds. Brian wouldn't be recording for the first time in ten years, and Brian wouldn't *even* be touring for the first fucking time in ten years if it weren't for Stephen. If it weren't for you, Stephen, the Beach Boys wouldn't be back on top and going to Russia to be the first American band to ever perform there! If it weren't for you, Brian *wouldn't even be here, period!*"

Sated, we left the restaurant and jumped into the limo. Stan looked at Stephen and continued, "And, I'll never forget that you're the one who asked Marilyn to give you a last chance to save Brian's life. If I ever forget that, Rocky, I want you to kick my ass."

I said, "Deal!"

Brian was moved. "They say *I'm* the wizard. I think *you're* the wizard for hiring Stan and Rocky—and saving my ass."

Marilyn gasped, "Wow! Now you're *really* blowing my mind, Brian."

I was in the front seat, driving, but I heard it all. "Brian, what about Marilyn? Doesn't she deserve any credit?"

I looked in the rearview mirror and caught a glimpse of Brian looking Marilyn in the eye for the first time in who knows how long. With the utmost sincerity, he said softly, "I owe you a great debt of gratitude and I apologize for . . . you know . . . for everything I did . . . and *didn't* do. You were always there for me, Marilyn. Thanks for not giving up on me."

Marilyn's eyes filled. "I never thought I'd hear anything like this from you, Brian."

"Must be the squab!" Brian joked.

Everyone cracked up. I cranked up the radio, and magically, as if on cue, we heard "Good Vibrations."

We all sang, "Good, good, good, good vibrations. . ." We laughed our asses off and continued singing, "She's giving me excitations . . ."

Brian turned the volume down on his back-seat radio controls so he could be heard, and sang exuberantly, "We're going on vacation!"

Marilyn, Stan, Stephen and I laughed at Brian's impromptu change of lyrics. Happy, Marilyn said, "If we hadn't just gone to lunch, I'd say let's go to the Luau."

"The hell with it. Let's go anyway!" I urged.

"Yeah, let's go, Marilyn," Stan said.

"Screw it. Let's go!" she directed.

Brian sang out, "We're already on vacation!"

Everyone in the back of the limo laughed. Beating Brian to the punch, Stan said, "And yes, Brian, you can have one grasshopper."

"No, wait. I want a mai tai this time. That's what *you* guys always have at the Luau."

"Okay, Brian," Stephen said, "I'll have a mai tai with you. It's my favorite Hawaiian drink. We'll celebrate the tremendous success we are having as a team."

"You hear that, Brian? We're a team," Stan laughed.

I added, "And you're the star quarterback of the team, Brian."

Brian smiled, "Must be the squab!"

Marilyn, Stephen, Stan and I cracked up, then we howled in unison, "Owoooooo!"

Chapter Seven

Wipeout

It was a good thing our Paris flight didn't leave until 10:00 p.m., for the mai tais were flowing at the Luau that afternoon and evening.

That is, the mai tais were flowing for everyone *but* Brian and Stephen, who each had a single drink. Stephen kept Brian entertained throughout the evening with stories about surfing, football, and college life at USC, and Marilyn, Stan, and I enjoyed ourselves without worrying about Brian for one carefree night. The three of us needed a break, and we always got along well.

We'd warned Stephen about the gross story I made up the year before when I first met Brian, so when Brian asked Stephen if he'd ever done the white t-shirt trick, Stephen denied it with a straight face.

Thank God, Stephen was also our designated driver, because we were pretty damn relaxed when we boarded the flight to Paris late that evening. The perks of flying first class were evident, and flutes of champagne were at the ready. Stan and I let the flight attendants know that under no circumstances was Brian to be served anything alcoholic.

Stan and I took turns napping during the long international

flight; one of us was always awake and on top of the situation with Brian. The next morning, we arrived in Paris without incident, passed through customs, and checked into the Hotel Ritz for one night.

Brian wanted to stay in the suite all day, but Marilyn, Stan, and I managed to get him out of the hotel to do some sightseeing. As happy tourists, we visited the Left Bank, where many renowned artists have painted a canvas or two and the street cafes are abundant and charming.

That night, Stan stayed in the suite with Brian and ordered room service, one of Brian's favorite treats. Marilyn and I were free to spend the evening together and enjoy a classic Parisian experience, so we dressed up and made reservations at the Ritz's renowned restaurant, L'Espadon. We enjoyed each other's company. Marilyn had not had fun like this in years, and the evening was surprisingly intoxicating for both of us.

We splurged on champagne and caviar for starters, then savored some exquisite garlicky escargots. We enjoyed a plate of carpaccio, and a special salad that was created at our table.

Marilyn and I ordered rare duck breast with foie gras and drank a magnificent French red wine with our entrées. For dessert, we ordered Crêpes Suzette and snifters of Grand Marnier.

The following day, the four of us flew into Nice, rented a luxury sedan, and made our way to St. Tropez. After we checked into the five-star Byblos Hotel, we relaxed and enjoyed the amazing views of the Mediterranean from our rooms. The next couple of days we spent doing what people on vacation do—sightseeing, sunbathing, shopping, dining out, and relaxing.

On the fourth day, Marilyn and I met for a casual lunch by the pool, just the two of us. Stan agreed to watch Brian in the

WIPEOUT

room, so we took our time. We were in the middle of a relaxed, happy meal when I thought I heard Brian's voice. A burst of laughter from the pool bar followed, and something sounded off kilter. I thought it wise to go investigate, so I excused myself and strode over to the bar.

A barefoot Brian was holding court at the bar, wearing pajamas—and he was high as a kite. I immediately knew that both drugs and alcohol were involved. Idiot fans had been generous enough to provide Brian with drinks, and, apparently, with some kind of psychedelic drug. Brian was tripping.

In the middle of a loud, nonsensical rant, Brian saw me and blurted, "What are you doing here, Rocky?"

"The better question is, what are *you* doing here, Brian?"

Brian started a laughing jag mixed with gibberish. I asked the crowd, "Can anyone tell me what drug he took?" I wasn't surprised when no one answered.

There was no doubt he must have taken a psychedelic of some kind. Clearly, a lot was going on in Brian's mind—something along the lines of experiencing his own personal tragicomedy, where the characters were all fragmented, and reality no longer existed. He was so into it, he was completely out of it, and he was fast coming to the point where he could no longer cope. In the one minute that I'd been in the bar, Brian deteriorated so fast that he was no longer making sense at all. It was sad. It was scary. It was horrific—and it was happening in real time.

Brian was splitting from himself, his mind was splintering into a million pieces, a kaleidoscope made of a myriad of fragmented particles scattering and changing colors, shapes and sizes in an endless stream of dazed confusion. The voices in Brian's head were all present and accounted for. He, on the other hand, was lost; he was somewhere out there in another dimension.

I didn't know what to do, other than wrap my arms around him. "Come on, Brian. Let's go." I escorted him back to his suite.

Stan was there, still damp from his shower, frantically getting dressed. "Thank God, Rocky! I got out of the shower and he was gone!"

"All right, stay with Brian," I directed, "while I get Marilyn and we figure out what to do."

Marilyn called the hotel doctor, who sedated an increasingly agitated Brian with Thorazine, Brian's favorite medication.

We dodged the silver bullet.

Marilyn wisely decided to cut the vacation short and head back to Los Angeles, where Brian was considerably safer. She knew being on the road was dangerous for Brian. He'd had his first breakdown on the road in 1964, and he was in London a couple years later when he had his second nervous breakdown.

At that time, the music scene was really changing. America was in the midst of the British Invasion: The Fab Four had eclipsed the Beach Boys, and the raunchier Rolling Stones were all the rage, as well as the U.S.-born Jimi Hendrix, whose band *Experience* emerged from the posh London club scene. That was just the beginning of the hard rock era.

The Beach Boys were in danger of becoming passé.

As an emotional and sensitive guy, the fear of being displaced affected Brian intensely and personally. Add the voices in his head to the mix, and it's a miracle he survived at all.

There is no business like the music business: It turns young, naïve unknowns into rich, famous people overnight. The cruel, balancing dynamic is when last year's flavor of the month gets chewed up, spit out, and left for dead next to roadkill.

The music business boneyard is full of the discarded, empty

shells of drug-addicted artists whose lives and minds are in chaos and disarray, spiraling out of control, their fall from the heights an endless drop into a bottomless abyss.

While Dennis and Carl partied like maniacs, trying like hell to dispel their soft, pop image, and earn a reputation as hard-edged, hip, rock stars, they were being betrayed by their very own fans, many of whom wouldn't admit that they once liked the Beach Boys. The harmonizing pop idols had suddenly become personae non gratae.

Marilyn, Brian, Stan, and I returned from Europe on Thursday evening. Stan called Stephen and told him we had returned early and safely. Stephen said quietly, "I need to stop by tomorrow to talk to all of you."

Stan shared Stephen's words with us, and Marilyn said, "While we were gone, lots of people called here, though they knew we were on vacation. It seems a little strange. People seem to know something I don't know. And it seems they all want to tell me."

Stephen arrived early the following afternoon, and he wasn't his usual casual, jovial self—he appeared preoccupied and slightly agitated. Without preamble, he said, "Can we talk in the office?" Once we were seated, he continued, "I'll get straight to the point. Mike has joined ranks with Carl and Dennis."

I had crossed paths with all three of them, not gently. I knew my time was up. "Uh oh. I get the feeling I'm not indispensable."

Marilyn spoke up. "They can't fire you, Rocky. You work for Brian and me."

Stephen said, flatly, "It's not *you* they're after, Rocky. It seems *I'm* the one they don't think is indispensable."

Marilyn, Stan, and I stared blankly at Stephen. He added, "They want to fire me."

"*What?!*" We three were in perfect harmony.

"They want to hold a vote tomorrow, and they want you to cast Brian's vote at the meeting, Marilyn."

"Well, they'll never get *my* vote to remove you, Stephen."

"Thank you, Marilyn. That means a great deal to me, but, unfortunately, they won't need your vote to get rid of me."

I thought back to Stephen's unfortunate telegram to Mike. This classic talent-management rift seemed to be of the terminal variety.

Stephen continued, "They have no idea what the repercussions will be. They think that because the tour is all set up, they don't need me. But I assure you, there is a very high probability that the entire tour could implode. And not because I would do or say anything to anybody, but simply by virtue of the fact that it is *my* signature on all the contracts with all forty of the individual concert promoters. When my name is removed from the contracts, the fallout could very well be disastrous. The entire tour could be canceled."

Exasperated, Stephen continued. "The last thing I said to them was that if the tour gets canceled, the *Beach Boys* could just as well be canceled."

Let's pause and put this in context.

The Beach Boys had been a near-defunct group. Brian was finally back, they were making records, and, at last, they were building some momentum. Now it was 1977, and they were poised to make a remarkable comeback with forty international concerts in twenty countries, from Russia to England to France to Germany to Italy and Scandinavia plus all the good concert venues on the map.

Wipeout

That Saturday, united for once, the Beach Boys insisted on calling for a corporate vote. By a 4-1 margin, Stephen was removed as manager, effective immediately. Marilyn voted for retention, as Brian's proxy.

Stephen left the band with his brilliant "Brian's Back" campaign and a shiny new recording contract still intact, but not for long.

Three days later, on a Tuesday morning with no one at the helm in the Beach Boys corporate office, the staff was inundated with phone calls and besieged with threatened lawsuits. On Friday, the band's worst nightmare occurred. As Marilyn predicted, the entire 40-date international tour was canceled and lawsuits were flying around like sea gulls at the beach.

Without Stephen, there was nobody to mind the store. Millions of dollars were lost in a financial fiasco with far-reaching consequences. Besides directly affecting the Beach Boys, dozens of promoters were on the hook. They had already advanced funds to secure concert venues, print tickets, and advertise the appearances, and they too were deemed culpable in a myriad of pending lawsuits.

Of course, there was substantial lost revenue from unsold tickets, but that money was nothing when compared to the ancillary money-making opportunities that had been there for the taking: record sales, paraphernalia (t-shirts, hats, etc.), and future tour bookings.

When the tour imploded, the repercussions blocked the career momentum Stephen had been building. The Beach Boys were now, more than ever, experiencing a wipeout. They were being pitched right off a monster wave, and they were very close to drowning.

Chapter Eight

Brian's Back

A couple of months later, after the tour had fully disintegrated and was a litigious hot mess, the Beach Boys called a desperation meeting. They reinstated Stephen as manager, with the hope that he could somehow miraculously "save the tour." It was too late; the damage had been done. A year's work was trashed.

The scuttlebutt being bantered around the mercurial, fickle music business was that the Beach Boys had become unreliable, which put Stephen in a difficult position. Booking the band was going to take delicate negotiations.

The band did as talent often does and passed the whole affair off as a misunderstanding, suggesting that Stephen only had to postpone things, to reschedule everything, and everything would be cool.

Hawaii was looking better to Stephen every day. He could imagine leaving it all behind and climbing onto a (real) surfboard. Instead, he spent the next six months waging a damage control campaign, trying to restore the band's credibility among leery concert promoters, and struggling with bookings for 1978.

Right after Stephen returned, the band traveled to London

to perform at the CBS Records convention, where all the label's major acts performed. Each artist showcased a portion of their forthcoming material in front of the company's rank and file.

Brian accompanied the Beach Boys, which was a big deal. Before the show, an awkward scene occurred backstage. Stan and I were escorting Brian, who was fretting over that night's show with the Beach Boys. Never a relaxed performer, he was nervous about performing live onstage in front of his new record company's executives, and Brian was a little jittery about how his new music would be received. As soon as we entered the restricted backstage lounge area, we saw a disheveled, inebriated James Taylor, smashed on his ass. James, recognizing Brian, rushed up to greet him with outstretched arms, but he stumbled and spilled his cocktail all over the front of Brian's tuxedo as he crashed into him.

Distracted and nervous, Brian had no idea who the klutz was. James was already in mid-sentence, apologizing and saying, "I'm a huge fan of yours, Brian!" Not hearing his words, Brian performed a sidestep spin and disappeared behind the curtain like a deft magician, leaving James wondering if he had just seen a mirage. Recognizing the awkwardness of the encounter, Stan stepped in, shook James Taylor's hand, and introduced himself as Brian's cousin. He explained that Brian suffers from shyness. James, dazed and confused, staggered off without saying a word, shaking his head.

Brian changed into a yellow-flowered Hawaiian shirt, cream colored linen slacks and a pair of white tennis shoes, sporting an elegant surf-and-sand look. I looked at Brian and thought to myself, "He sure has cleaned up his act from when I first laid eyes on him."

I smiled warmly at Brian, "You look great, Calypso Joe." Brian looked down at his attire and gave me a shy, awkward, half smile. I added with a grin, "That was a hell of a nifty football spin move you put on James Taylor back there."

Brian tilted his head to one side and exclaimed, "*That* was James Taylor?"

I laughed. "You see what booze and who-knows-what-drugs will do to you!"

When the Beach Boys were introduced as America's all-time favorite band from southern California, featuring the one and only, the incomparable Brian Wilson, the crowd erupted in a standing ovation that lasted for at least three solid minutes. Mike Love, the savvy showman that he is, realized the applause was for Brian and he held the band back. He knew this was good for the whole band.

Brian walked to the microphone at center stage, looking like the athletic, clean-cut teenager he once was, tall and lean, with his bass slung over his shoulder. Waiting for the applause to subside, jittery and uncomfort-

The "Brian's Back" effect is now in full bloom and Brian has slimmed down to a trim 190 pounds. Animated and playing bass like a teenager, Brian is again doing what he loves, and he's doing it better than most.

*Photo by Stan Love
from the Larry Salisbury Collection*

able, he waved and flashed a nervous smile.

When the roar died down, Brian blurted out, "I want to dedicate this song to Stan and Rocky, two of the coolest guys." Without hesitating, he did a quick countdown and launched into a song.

Stan and I were stunned. No, *shocked* is a better word, to be perfectly honest. Stan had told me a year before, "Don't *ever* think that we will get thanked by these guys. It's a foreign concept to them."

I shook Stan's hand and said, "Look, we said in the beginning this isn't about thanks—it's about saving Brian's life."

"Yeah, you're right. At least Brian knows we're trying to save his life. We're actually appreciated." Stan was solemn.

The Beach Boys' mini-performance was concluding, and, to everyone's amazement, the entire audience of recording executives and bigwigs jumped to its feet and erupted again in a thunderous standing ovation that lasted at least five full minutes.

And then something very interesting occurred. People started chanting *Brian's back, Brian's back*, again and again. And just when you thought it couldn't go on any longer, Stan and I pushed Brian back out onstage for a lone curtain call and the crowd went wild. Over and over, they screamed, *We love you, Brian! We love you, Brian!*

Brian was astounded and overwhelmed. He bowed his head for a very long time, then wiped a tear from his eye, waved to the audience, and humbly made his way offstage.

That did not stop the overwhelming applause. I looked around and saw Stephen with his head bowed. I could have sworn I saw a tear trickling down his cheek, too. Stephen was responsible for this. He orchestrated this comeback. The

Brian's Back

"Brian's Back" campaign was his brainchild, and it was now officially nothing less than an off-the-charts, phenomenal success—not just because of the monster recording contract Stephen negotiated for the Beach Boys—but, more significantly, because he deserved credit for saving the life of one of the greatest songwriters the world has ever known, his cousin Brian.

Even Paul McCartney reveres Brian Wilson. It's a well-known fact. When asked by *Rolling Stone* magazine what kind of music he listens to, Paul responded, "I don't have much time to listen to music, but when I do it's usually on the way to or from the airport. I usually stop and buy a new copy of Brian Wilson's conceptual masterpiece, *Pet Sounds*. I think the majestic single "God Only Knows" is perhaps the greatest pop song ever written."

This is perhaps the greatest compliment ever paid by rock and roll royalty, the embodiment of which is Sir Paul McCartney.

Backstage, Stephen, Stan and I were chilling out in a quiet corner. Brian was looking very uncomfortable surrounded by VIPs and label execs. When he spotted the three of us, he made a beeline over to our corner and asked, "Can we go now?"

Stan said, tongue in cheek, "Not a bad show, Brian."

"You were *great*, Brian!" Stephen said with emphasis.

I chimed in, "You hear that, Brian? They're still clapping and chanting '*We love you, Brian.*' That's what I call pure love—and it's all for *you*, Brian."

Brian turned to Stephen, "I want to thank you for hiring these guys. And thanks for not allowing me to fire them."

Stephen blushed. "Well, cuz, what are friends for?"

Brian was tired. "Can we go now?"

Stephen affectionately put his arm around Brian's shoulders and murmured, "Sure, Brian, but why don't you say goodbye to all these nice people first?"

Brian said sweetly, to no one in particular, "'Bye, everyone." He turned to Stephen. "Why don't you come with us, okay?"

Walking to the limo, Stan said facetiously, "You know, they ought to have a Hall of Fame for people who save the lives of rock stars."

I opened the limo door. Brian jumped in and chuckled, "Yeah, but there wouldn't be very many. Too many rocks stars are dead."

Stan agreed. "That's true—Elvis, Jimi Hendrix, Janis Joplin, Jim Morrison—those were some of the greats. And they're all gone now. Yeah, rock stars are a handful. They're a bunch of freakin' prima donnas, if you ask me."

Brian smiled, "Stan, you can call me a freakin' prima donna if you want, but just don't call me late for dinner!" He paused for a beat, then asked on cue, "Can I have a steak sandwich when we get back to the hotel?"

"Just one," Stan and I said in unison that being a running gag between us. When we got back to the hotel, Brian practically sprinted to his suite so he could get on the phone and order his beloved room-service steak sandwich. Stan did his best to keep up with Brian as he raced to the room.

Sauntering along with Stephen, I confided, "You should have seen your face during Brian's curtain call. You had a look on your face I'll never forget. I *saw* it, Stephen. You know that song 'The Look of Love,' by Dusty Springfield? Well, you had that look, my friend. It looked good on ya, man."

A modest person, Stephen was silent, obviously uncomfortable.

"It's all right, Stephen, you don't have to say anything.

Besides, we've got to get up tomorrow and do it all over again."

"You're right about that, Rocky. Tonight was a landmark experience, but you can never let your guard down with these guys. They're as unpredictable as the day is long."

Chapter Nine

A Year into Our Gig

Reprise Records released *The Beach Boys Love You*, their final Beach Boys album, just eleven days after Stephen was fired; it included many of the tracks that Brian had recorded late the previous year, when Stan and I got him up and into the studio regularly. Though the album got great reviews from other musicians and critics, Reprise barely promoted it, and Stephen wasn't there to hold them to their agreement.

CBS waited to start their own Beach Boys marketing campaign until the Reprise album fell off the charts (which it did pretty quickly). CBS knew they wanted the perfect music journalist to interview the reclusive Brian in person.

CBS presented the interview idea to Brian, and an executive suggested he work with top writers from Rolling Stone, its British equivalent, Melody Maker, or several other well-known music magazines. Brian refused them all, saying unequivocally, "I'll do an interview with Dick Clark!"

The legendary Dick Clark wasn't on the table. The CBS executive paused and said, "Well, um, I'll see if we can get him. He really hasn't conducted any interviews lately, you realize, Brian."

Brian smiled, "Neither have I. Get Dick and I'll do the

interview. Tell him we can do it here at my house—and *then* call me."

The interview was set up for the following Wednesday at 4:00 p.m.

Dick Clark showed up for the interview at precisely 4:00 o'clock, looking about 20 years old. Marilyn gave him a warm greeting, explained that Brian was by the pool, and introduced Stan and me as Brian's trainers and personal assistants. We told Dick what an honor it was to meet him.

Dick came prepared; he knew what we'd been doing with Brian. He asked us, "Is it true that Brian is way down from 300 pounds?"

We said in unison, "Yes."

"And he's actually going to tour on a regular basis?"

"Yes, he is!"

"I see you two work as a team," Dick said. "Great job!"

"Come on, we'll take you to Brian," Stan said. "He's more excited than we've seen him in a long time. He's been telling people about this interview for days now—and how he's kind of nervous because he says you never age, it's been awhile since he's seen you, and how you are the only one he would allow to do a personal interview. He says you're a real pro."

We escorted him to the pool, and as we were about to leave him with Brian, Marilyn arrived with a pitcher of lemonade and two glasses on a tray. She put the tray on the patio table in the shade, and the three of us left so the two legends could talk privately.

Curiosity quickly got the best of Stan and me, and we lurked around the corner—within earshot and out of sight.

We heard Brian say to Dick, "When the Beatles came on the scene in '63, it was like, *wow*, these guys are good. What a sound! I mean they had a really good sound. The minute I heard their voices, I just flipped my lid. When I heard Paul sing 'I Wanna Hold Your Hand,' when I heard that sustained note on *hand*, I just lost it. Man, that was a moment I'll never forget. And I decided right then and there that I wanted to write an album that was as good as the Beatles', one that could compete with the Beatles. So, I started writing *Pet Sounds* because that's what everyone kept telling me to do, and that's what the Beatles' music made me do.

"Stan was a pro basketball player. He's tall and strong. And Rocky was a pro football player. He's a real big, strong guy, too. Stephen hired them for me. They're really protective of me. I know I'm safe when I'm with them. Stan is my first cousin, and Rocky was Stan's roommate and best friend in college. I played football, too, you know; in high school. I was a quarterback. My other cousin Stephen played football in high school, too. So, the four of us have that sports thing in common. Stan and Rocky and I play basketball five days a week at the gym. We always win. Sometimes we throw the football around too. I can still pass pretty good and they can catch everything. We have that athlete thing going on."

Dick was quiet for a beat. "That sounds good, Brian. That sounds really good. I'm glad you have some guys around that you can trust and have something in common with outside of music. And what's especially great is the fact that they make you feel so safe."

"Oh yeah. I know they've got my back. They would never let anyone touch me."

"That's great, Brian. They seem like good guys. The CBS people speak highly of them also.

Stan and I heard enough. We thought back over the last

year, and how far Brian had come.

Brian looked, smelled, and sounded great. He was in good physical shape, thanks to our successful exercise regime and the fact that Marilyn had put locks on their 10-foot-wide refrigerator. Brian had short, neatly trimmed hair and was clean-shaven. His toes were pedicured and his hands were manicured. His mood was stable, thanks to his psychiatrist tweaking his schizophrenia medications. He felt safe and comfortable with Stan and me, and he seemed to be happy.

We'd recently had him tested at a sports medicine facility where he was put through all types of tests, some cardiovascular, others checking his muscle mass. He was down to 195 pounds and in pretty good shape, with 23 percent body fat—not bad for a guy who'd lost over 100 pounds.

After the testing, Brian surprised us by asking to go to a track and really jog. The three of us ran side-by-side for a mile, and he still had some reserves. I was surprised but happy when Brian asked to throw the football around. He played quarterback, Stan flanked out to the wide receiver position, and I hiked the ball to Brian and ran pass routes.

Brian was *damn* good. His accuracy and timing were excellent; he knew how to lead the receiver, and the velocity he put on the ball was surprising. Brian had a real zip to his passes. Maybe all those years of playing piano and bass gave him extra strength in his wrists and arms. I know his forearms felt like rocks from our basketball scrimmages.

He had fun that day, and it was hard to get him away from the football field. Brian was like a kid in the candy store, grinning from ear to ear.

Equally important, his mind was in a good place, too. He'd always been an eccentric, walking around with his mind somewhere else, lost in music and deeply preoccupied. Of course, Brian's brain had been affected by that lost decade on drugs, as well as the other mental health issues that he had.

Still, Stan and I had watched Brian's ability to deal with business and decisions evolve over the last year.

Stephen would drive over to get Brian's signature on various pieces of paperwork, and Brian could stay lucid for a while before he reverted to his distracted and preoccupied state of mind. He would listen intently to what Stephen had to say and respond—clear as a bell—in a remarkably succinct way. He demonstrated the ability to reduce things to their essence and he made it clear he had a complete grasp of the subject at hand.

Brian was back, in more ways than one, and it was incredibly rewarding to those of us who loved him, especially to his cousin Stephen. Stan and I took a lot of credit for the turnaround, but we knew Stephen was ultimately responsible.

Chapter Ten

Brian's Christmas Gift

The repercussions from the canceled international concert tour were expensive for everyone involved.

Reprise Records suffered from the blowback; they had geared up for a major promotion and their marketing and sales division had flooded the record stores in every tour city with tons of their Beach Boys product. The executives were furious.

CBS was pissed, because the fallout had hurt the Beach Boys brand they'd just paid millions for. Walter Yetnikoff, the president of CBS Records, pondered the $2 million advance that he'd paid to the band, and pronounced in dismay, "I think I have been fucked!" Not exactly what you want the head of your new record label to say.

The concert promoters were equally enraged, as they had fronted serious money to book performance venues, print tickets, and launch their own individual advertising campaigns. Now the Beach Boys found themselves ensnarled in a whole slew of pending lawsuits. The sharks were circling.

The saddest consequence from the cancellation was that the tour would have been a badly-needed success, generating millions in concert ticket and record sales. The Beach Boys have always had exceptionally strong album sales in the European market, and some of the band's most ardent fans resided there.

This was a terrible blow for a group that was anything but solvent. Having been metaphorically beached to begin with, they were now truly wiped out. Their status within the music business was that of a pariah, their reputation in tatters and seemingly beyond repair.

To hold their losses to a minimum, CBS Records demanded delivery of the first album that the band owed them, as spelled out in the new contract. CBS insisted that the band deliver their songs by the end of the year, and further stipulated that there would be *no* extensions or leeway. The record executives were pissed, and they had no intention of yielding.

There was a problem.

Brian had written nothing—*nada*—no songs whatsoever since early that year. He had counted on being granted an extension by his new label. With the honeymoon most definitely over, and the relationship strained, any possibility of an extension was out of the question.

Potentially career-threatening lawsuits were looming. It wasn't outside the realm of possibility to suppose that CBS Records just might arrive at the conclusion that these guys were too much trouble and they should be dropped. The label already had several top-selling artists on its roster and was doing just fine.

Problems were arising on the domestic tour front, too; several large venues in the States were pulling out and promoters were getting skittish. It took all of Stephen's managerial skill to keep things on track. Even then, he was only able to book smaller venues for the remainder of 1977—colleges and

Brian's Christmas Gift

universities—a risky proposition in terms of credibility and image.

There was one ray of light—Stephen's proposal for the yet-unwritten album. He came up with a compromise, recommending that the group record a Christmas album, traditional standards that Brian could arrange in his unique style, and that wouldn't require him to write a dozen songs. It was a neat solution and could be a lucrative boon to CBS Records in the long run, because Christmas albums sell year after year and are known for being perennial moneymakers.

The band resisted. They must have hoped that Brian would pull off a miracle.

Brian normally didn't take part in the band's meetings; instead, he left it to Marilyn to listen to what was going on and vote on his behalf. But this time was different. Since his vacation meltdown, something had changed inside Brian. He was almost leery of drugs, and he even expressed some concern about the future.

Brian entered his family room, interrupted the meeting, and said flatly, "I don't have any songs written. Stephen's idea for a Christmas album is brilliant. Remember when Aunt Glee had us sing at her Christmas caroling parties? So, if you guys aren't 'all in,' you're 'all out,' and I'll do it myself. Get it? And there's *not* going to be a vote."

On that note, Brian slammed his fist down hard on the white baby grand piano resting in the middle of his family room/beach, and declared, "This meeting is *adjourned!*" He walked briskly out of the room without waiting to hear another word.

Stunned, Marilyn followed her new hero out of the room as she proudly announced, "Brian's back!"

Stan and I were in the office, listening intently to Brian's miraculous diatribe. When Brian walked by, Stan whispered, "Psst! Brian!"

Brian quickly slipped into the office, closed the door behind him, and asked, "So how did I do?"

Stan and I put our arms around Brian. Stan said, "Brian, you're the greatest!"

I added, "Brian, you're our hero."

Grinning from ear to ear, Brian joked, "I was just aiming for Man of the Hour. I guess I outdid myself."

Stan agreed, "Yes, Brian. Wait till we tell Stephen what you just did."

Marilyn opened the door, walked in, looked at Stan and me, and asked, "Did you hear Brian?"

We said, "Yeah!"

Brian picked up the phone. "Dial Stephen's number. I want to tell him myself."

Stephen answered his phone. "Hello?"

"Stephen, this is Brian. I love your idea for a Christmas album. The other guys said they didn't like the idea, but I put my foot down and insisted we do it. Why don't you come over for dinner tonight? The guys are just leaving."

"I'll be over right after my workout."

Marilyn looked at Brian, and, with a huge smile on her face, said, "You were *amazing*, Brian. We're going to the Luau!"

Before Stephen came over that evening, he went to the beach for some exercise. He's a versatile athlete, and beach volleyball had become his favorite pastime. Stephen lived in a charming little town south of the Los Angeles airport, Manhattan Beach. His house, 100 The Strand, was just up from the northern edge of Hermosa Beach. The suntanned bodies of the most beautiful girls in the world paraded up and down the promenade in their revealing bikinis outside his front door, and the best beach volleyball players in the southland were within walking distance. He didn't have to go far to get up a game with his outstanding partner, Don Braunecker. Don was an AA player; Stephen was an A player, but he spent most of his time playing against AAs.

The South Bay beach scene was surreal, a paradise of sorts. You had scantily clad gorgeous girls strutting about showing off their tans and fit bodies, and you had all these good-looking volleyball players performing in their baggy shorts and sun visors and nothing else but the sweat on their athletic, sun-tanned bodies. The imagery conveyed to the world by Beach Boys songs was personified by the southern California lifestyle.

Many of Stephen's friends, in fact, referred to him as "a beach boy," and this was before he took up surfing. Surfing came later—it was too time-intensive to practice while handling the full-time job of managing the Beach Boys.

A word or two about beach volleyball is in order here. The sport had become one of the most talked about and exciting sports in America, and quickly became an Olympic sport as well as a professional one. Near the many sand courts on the beach, you'd often hear "Catch a Wave," "Warmth of the Sun," "The Girls on the Beach" or any number of Beach Boys songs playing in the background.

The backdrop to all this activity was, I repeat, surreal. You had the sun shining all the time, the breezes blowing, the crashing of waves on the shore, the sight of surfers carving waves and paddling back out to do it again, bicyclists cruising up and down the strand, sunbathers throwing their Frisbees and making their diving catches in the soft sand, toddlers wading in the shallow water under a parent's watchful eye, waves lapping on the shore, the seagulls gliding and soaring and yakking in the wind, and of course the many couples strolling hand in hand along the endless shoreline.

This was the environment Stephen and his live-in girlfriend, Mary Newland, enjoyed. Being the girlfriend of the Beach Boys' manager gave Mary status among her girlfriends. Stephen was a celebrity at Rosecrans, the famous California volleyball beach. Stephen was truly living what the Beach Boys sang about—even if *they* weren't—and he was loving it!

Stephen finished playing a couple of spirited volleyball matches with the great Don Braunecker, went home, and showered and shaved before heading up to Brian's place to join Brian, Marilyn, Stan and me for a celebratory dinner.

In October, the Beach Boys traveled to the Maharishi International University (MIU) in Fairfield, Iowa, with their portable recording studio, and they recorded the new Christmas album.

While we were isolated in the wilds of Iowa, Mike asked that the Maharishi Mahesh Yogi's videotaped Transcendental Meditation lectures be made available to the Beach Boys and their crew of support technicians and musicians. No one except Mike took much interest in the tapes, though Marilyn and I attended the first video session with Mike, his female companion at the time, and Al Jardine.

We were underwhelmed; no one but Mike and Al took much interest. The tape consisted of a twenty-minute lecture by the diminutive Indian guru, who had a very high-pitched voice and a most peculiar sense of humor, as he sat atop a stack of pillows. Following the lecture there was a twenty-minute meditation. Instead of closing my eyes and meditating I ended up watching the Maharishi breathe for twenty minutes; it was hard to resist the temptation to sneak a peek at the little dude.

Later, I told Marilyn and Stan, "If that's what meditation, serenity, and peace of mind are supposed to look like, Mike can have it! It's a damn good thing the session only lasted forty minutes. I don't know how much more I could have taken."

I'm glad Mike didn't hear me put down his beloved Maharishi, because later he did something really generous—he volunteered to teach me how to sing background harmonies on a song they recorded.

First, he said, "No vibrato." I asked him to sing the eight-bar background so I could hear exactly what he wanted. He did, then I asked if we could sing it together. The third time around, I sang it solo, and Mike said, "That's good!" I had to admit, maybe there is something to that meditation thing after all.

To my delight, Mike recorded me singing the background to that Christmas album song along with Marilyn and her sister Diane. When I finished, I thanked Mike and added, "Now I know why Brian says you're such a great singer."

It was almost worth sitting through another meditation with the Maharishi. *Almost.*

Chapter Eleven

Barefootin'

After he was given his job back that summer, Stephen remained intensely aware of the fallout from the 40-date international tour implosion—fallout both to the Beach Boys' reputation and to their finances. He was faced with the gargantuan task of picking up the pieces and trudging forward—or upward and onward, as he said without bitterness.

Looking ahead to 1978, he worked on a three-week jaunt Down Under to Australia and New Zealand, and he negotiated a badly needed $250,000 advance. The guy running the show was none other than David Frost, the famous TV star who was just beginning a very successful second career as a concert promotor and producer.

In addition to the cash advance, we were given two dozen round trip airline tickets, half of which were first class, to be used by the band members, spouses, and management.

Stephen called the group together for a meeting on Brian's patio, and he explained the tour's workings to the guys. Brian tapped him on the shoulder and asked if he could have a few moments of Stephen's time. It was clear that something was on his mind, and Stephen excused himself and joined Brian in his den.

Brian couldn't quite meet his eyes. "Steve, you know I don't like to travel much and Australia is a long way away. Do I *have* to go on this tour?"

Stephen knew he just had to be straight with him. "Yes, Brian. Your participation is one of the key elements of the deal. David Frost insisted. The tour is going to be a big money-maker, and the fans down under are dying to see you."

Brian understood. It was important. "Okay, I'll go!" And that was that.

Meanwhile, being the practical manager that he was, Stephen made sure he got us back on the road as soon as possible. He arranged a modest six-date tour of Midwest colleges and universities to follow our Christmas album sessions.

The highlight of the tour was our gig at the University of Notre Dame. On the Saturday afternoon before our concert, Stephen was comped 50-yardline seats to a Notre Dame home football game, and he took Brian, Stan, and me to the game. Brian hadn't been to a football game since he played in high school; he looked like a kid on Christmas morning. The four of us had a blast.

Our performance at Notre Dame was memorable, too. We had a sold-out appearance in the cavernous Fighting Irish basketball arena, a surprise smash with the young audience, and the overflow crowd of students went nuts.

Unfortunately, the rest of the tour was a sobering experience for the band, so to speak. We played before mostly small crowds, and the band felt the sting of the humiliation. The group should have been playing 20,000-seat arenas and the occasional soccer stadium in the capitals of Europe, and if it weren't for the ill-timed firing of their manager, that's exactly what they would have been doing.

What stuck in our craw was missing the opportunity to play Leningrad and be the first group to introduce the Soviet Union to western rock and roll. It would have been fantastic to be American ambassadors to Russia!

Instead, we were ambassadors to the Corn Belt. The last of the small Midwest shows took place at the University of Illinois in Champaign. There must be something in the air or water in Illinois that makes sure at least one of the Wilson brothers becomes inebriated before a performance. We were doubly unlucky this fall; both Carl and Dennis showed up drunk on their asses at this concert.

Why the Wilson brothers couldn't wait to party until *after* the show is a mystery no one has been able to unravel. I'm not sure either of them had a clue, either. Jim Morrison of the Doors captured the concept best, "I have the soul of a clown. That always makes me blow it at just the right time!"

Halfway through the gig, Carl fell backwards into the drum kit, scattering drums, cymbals, and his brother Dennis, ass over teakettle in all directions. It was a spectacle that did not go unappreciated by the college students, and laughter and boos reverberated throughout the seven-thousand-seat auditorium.

With the help of three strong roadies, Carl struggled to his feet. He tried to cover his ass when he apologized to the audience. "I tripped on a 'lectrical cord."

A fan in the front row yelled, "Your breath could start an electrical *fire!*"

Carl yelled back, "Fuck you, asshole!" It was a good thing he was slurring his words so badly, because the crowd couldn't make out what he said.

The roadies helped Dennis get up, but he never made it back to his scattered drum kit. He wandered off to get more booze and whatever other crap he could get his hands on. Our reliable back-up drummer, Mike Kowalski, swung into action once more.

Before things veered off-track any more, a sober and steady Mike Love stepped up to the mike and steered the show through to the end. It still wasn't one of the band's better moments, and some of the students left before the end of the show.

That night after the show, we traveled to a Chicago airport hotel. The flight home was scheduled for 10:00 a.m. the next day, and since our hotel was right at the airport, we felt we could sleep in a little, at last. But when Stan rolled out of bed at 8:00, Brian was gone. Panicked, Stan dashed next door and woke me, moaning frantically, "Brian's gone! Get dressed fast and let's check the nearest bar."

We sprinted to the bar—no sign of Brian. Stan asked the bartender, "Has anyone dressed in a green Adidas sweat suit been here the last hour or so?"

"Yeah, there was a guy in a green sweat suit. He stood out because he was barefoot—and because he puked all over my bar. He was sitting next to some guy who was buying him grasshoppers with an extra shot of vodka. After two of those, your guy barfed on the counter, which I had just wiped down. So, I told your guy he had to leave. He's lucky I didn't call security. But the guy buying him the drinks did say he was a Beach Boy and escorted him out of here. I heard this guy saying to your guy, 'Why don't you come on the flight with me?' Your guy said 'Okay.'"

Stan asked, "Did he say where he was going?"

The bartender was irritated, "No, and I don't fucking care."

Stan gave the guy twenty bucks. "Sorry. Don't tell anyone, okay?"

Barefootin'

We ran to the nearest arrival/departure screen; the next outbound flight was headed for Minneapolis, Minnesota, and it was taking off in a few minutes. We had to act fast. Stan said to me, "You get to that gate. I'll go to the main terminal and see if anyone bought a ticket in Brian's name."

I sprinted to the departure gate, and it was closed—the plane had just left. Though I was out of breath and spouting a bizarre story, when I gasped I was looking for a barefoot guy, the gate attendant came to life. She said, "Oh my God! There *was* a barefoot guy. He's on the plane! Who is he?"

I managed, "He's Brian Wilson of the Beach Boys and the guy who bought him the ticket is an absolute stranger he met in the airport bar, someone who's just bought him drinks. You've *got* to stop that plane and let me get him off, otherwise a really damaged guy will be lost in Minneapolis in the dead of winter—barefoot!"

Even though the airplane had pulled away from the ramp, the concerned gate attendant made a call, stopped the plane from taxiing out any further, and then took me downstairs and out onto the tarmac. The baggage handlers manually maneuvered a portable staircase into place, and I boarded the plane.

Meanwhile, Stan was at the main terminal, explaining that he was Beach Boy Brian Wilson's cousin, and he needed to know if a ticket had been purchased in that name. The ticket agent checked, and yes, a one-way ticket had been purchased in Brian's name for a flight to Minneapolis, but the plane was already taxiing out to the runway.

Stan begged, "*Please* stop that plane! My cousin is with a weird stranger, going to Minnesota, in the dead of winter, and he's barefoot!" and he dashed to the departure gate.

By that time, I had boarded the plane. I strode down the

center aisle, and easily spotted Brian in an aisle seat about twenty rows back. He looked up. "Rocky, what are you doing here?"

"Well, Brian, the real question is, what are *you* doing here?"

"I'm going with this guy."

Exuding the patience and calm of an elementary school teacher, I asked, mainly for the benefit of the nearby passengers, "Brian, do you even know the name of this guy who was buying you drinks in the airport bar for the last hour?"

Brian turned to his new friend and asked, "What's your name?" The guy didn't answer.

I asked, still calm, "Do you even know where you're going, Brian?"

Brian asked the guy, "Where are we going?" The stranger didn't meet his eyes or answer.

"Brian, you're on a plane going to Minneapolis in the dead of winter with a total stranger. And— you're barefoot." This drew a pretty big laugh; everyone within earshot was chuckling by this time. I cleared my throat, spoke up to make sure I had everyone's full attention, and addressed the man who had absconded with Brian. "You know, pal, you just made my job extremely difficult. I'm on Beach Boy Brian Wilson's personal staff. He needs constant surveillance because he suffers from," I lowered my voice to a whisper, "a temporary condition—if you get my drift." Nearby passengers got real quiet.

"You know, I can understand you buying a celebrity a drink in a bar even if it is only 7:00 a.m. and even after he threw up at the bar, but what I *can't* understand is why you would buy him a one-way ticket to your hometown just because you think it would be cool to be seen hanging out with a Beach Boy— especially one who is barefoot."

Barefootin'

Passengers were pointing and whispering. The guy was slinking down so low in his seat that it was obvious he was trying to make himself invisible. I threw in one last jab. "You know, *some* people might interpret your actions as a kidnapping. Now come on, Brian, let's go, shall we?"

Brian said half-heartedly, "I'm not going with you; I'm going with this guy."

The guy finally spoke up. "No, you're not!"

"Let's go, Brian."

I waited a beat. Brian said meekly, "Okay."

As he stood up to deplane, I said, "Say goodbye to your friend, Brian."

Without even turning to look back at the guy, Brian muttered a curt "Bye," and continued walking.

As we walked down the aisle, a passenger, parroting the lyrics to "Surfin' USA," sang "Everybody's gone barefootin'."

I laughed, "Not in Minnesota in the dead of winter, bro!"

Brian, the gate attendant, and I re-entered the airport and were greeted by a breathless Stan. "Thank God, you got him! How did you get them to stop the plane and let you on?"

"I think it was the desperation in my voice when I said to this nice lady that Brian Wilson, of the Beach Boys, is on that plane with a weird stranger and he's barefoot. That's when she said, 'Oh my God! There *was* a guy who was barefoot!'"

I turned to the gate attendant, and smiled, "So you, my charming lady, have saved Brian Wilson of sunny southern California from getting frostbite, and Brian would like to thank you."

Brian mumbled, "Thanks."

I added appreciatively, "This would not have been good for Brian or for us. You saved our butts."

The gate attendant smiled sweetly. "Well, our motto *is* 'Service with a smile.'"

I grinned. "I always thought it was coffee, tea—or me?"

She giggled, "Well, that too."

The three of us walked back to the hotel suite. Stan slammed the door, poked Brian in the chest, hard, and asked sarcastically, "Well, Brian, is frostbite an experience you wanna have?"

I was shocked at the poke because I'd never seen Stan touch Brian like that before, but it *was* a pretty good question.

Stan wasn't finished.

"Jesus Christ, *Minnesota*, in the dead of winter, *barefoot*, with a freaking stranger—just for some *drinks*?" (Even better.) "Are you out of your *mind*, Brian? You are certifiable. You know that, *don't* you?" (That was a bit rough.) "Wait until Marilyn finds out about this."

"You can't tell her," Brian pleaded. "She'll have me committed!" (Here we go again.)

I chimed in. "Oh, you know, we're *going* to tell her, Brian. There's no negotiating. You're kind of like a terrorist, only the person you're terrorizing is, unfortunately, yourself. Are a few drinks really worth the risk?"

Stan added, "And what about *us*, Brian? She's probably going to be pissed at us for almost losing you."

I pointed out, "Not as pissed as she'll be if she finds out we didn't tell her. If we're lucky she might realize that we saved the day and averted a possible tragedy. Not only did we save her husband from getting lost in Minnesota and receiving untold amounts of drugs and booze from strangers, but we saved him from possible frostbite, as you pointed out, Stan."

I looked Brian in the eyes, and said, sincerely, "You know, Brian, we love you. But what Stan and I just don't get is—your

BAREFOOTIN'

life is about *performing*, singing the beautiful uplifting songs you created. Songs that I can only imagine you created to give the world something to enjoy, something to make people's' lives a little better, even if only for a few hours out of their routine, tiresome days.

"Now tell me honestly, Brian. Is performing in front of tens of thousands of cheering fans that are screaming *We love you* and all that applause and adulation really *all* that hard to contend with? Singing your wonderful songs to the world is your gift! Do you know how many people would give everything they have for your gift of music, your gift of song? Don't you see how lucky you are, Brian? You are truly one of the chosen ones."

Brian was not his typical shut-off self during this appeal. He seemed somewhat moved. It was as though he understood that millions of people would *love* to be him, if only for a day—hell, even for an hour, or for the time it took to sing one song.

Stan, trying to be funny, said, "I just hope you're right, Rocky, and Marilyn doesn't have him committed."

"Oh, I think she'll see things my way in the end," I said, optimistically.

When we got back to Bel Air and walked into the mansion, Marilyn was waiting. Brian slunk right past her without so much as a hello.

I said, "Come, I'll fill you in on the latest," and opened a bottle of champagne. "Fortification. You're gonna need it!" I filled two flutes, clinked my glass with hers, and with a grin, said, "Cheers! By the way, we missed you. How are things in Bel Air? How was your shopping? It's a tough job, I know, but someone's got to do it. So, are the girls behaving? And I must say, you look fabulous. Have you been working out?"

Marilyn laughed at me and my lame preamble. "Okay, cut the shit and let me have it."

"Oh, I will, but first: bottoms up!"

"*What?*" Marilyn shrieked a few moments later, after listening to my tale. Her roar filled the office. In the end, she did see things as I had hoped she would. In fact, she decided that Brian's protectors deserved Christmas bonuses. On Christmas morning, Stan received a new set of Halliburton luggage and a red and green envelope containing a generous amount of cash.

I, too, received a generous amount of cash in a festive Christmas envelope. Combined with a healthy chunk of my savings, the money was enough to buy my almost-dream car, a used Mercedes SL convertible.

Within a few days, I bought the car I had been keeping my eyes on and drove it straight back to Bel Air.

"Come on, let's go for a spin." I led Marilyn to the passenger door, opened it and said, "After you."

As I walked to the other side, Stan said, "Take your time, bro. I've got things under control here."

I nodded, "See ya in about an hour."

"You got it!"

I still remember what a great car it was. There's nothing like eight cylinders with 4.5 liters of raw German-engineered power under you, the top down and the wind in your hair on a brisk winter day in sunny southern California, as you cruise down Sunset Boulevard in an almost-new car with a lovely lady by your side. Life is good.

I howled, "Owoooooo!"

Section II: 1978

Chapter Twelve

Dirty Deeds Down Under

The saga of our trip Down Under gives you a peek at the load of anxiety and frustration that Stephen, Stan, and I carried as we did our damnedest to keep Brian drug-free—while others threw monkey wrenches into the works.

We really needed this tour after our 40-date European tour fell apart in 1977 after Stephen was fired. After he was rehired by the band, Stephen spent the better part of six months negotiating a three-week whirlwind tour of Australia and New Zealand in conjunction with famous talk-show host David Frost's new venture into concert promoting.

The Down Under tour began in late February, 1978 in New Zealand and continued in Australia until mid-March. This was a *big* tour, with all the major cities on the itinerary, and Brian's presence was mandatory.

The concert dates were sold out for every venue, and attendance records were broken at several. Before the Beach Boys' tour, no rock-and-roll band had ever sold out two consecutive nights at the huge outdoor venue in Sydney. The sellout was even more impressive because it rained like hell one of those nights. As Stephen watched from the wings, he worried the guitarists would be electrocuted.

We came away from the flooded event with the appreciation for the Aussies' hardiness. Despite the downpour, not one person in the crowd of 25,000 left early, and the enthralled audience kept dancing and screaming and singing along with the Beach Boys the entire night. Australia loves the Beach Boys; New Zealand too, for that matter.

To say this major tour was a resounding success would be an understatement. Still, we had more than our share of embarrassments, high drama, a near-death experience, and some permanent repercussions. I think that Stephen, Stan, and I each lost a few years of our lives.

We had our first rocky bit when the band landed in Auckland, just a few hours into the tour. As we walked through the sleepy, quiet airport, Dennis and his wife created a major disturbance when they had one of their infamous, rip-roaring fights en route to the baggage claim.

His wife threw Dennis' shoes at his head, over and over, as she cursed him at the top of her lungs, using every profane word in her considerable vocabulary. The shoes bounced off his skull and shoulders, and she picked them up and threw them again. Dennis walked along, barefoot, handsome in a beautiful new light linen suit, pretending to be oblivious to it all, probably hoping bystanders wouldn't think her screams and curses were directed at him. It was slapstick comedy, right out of a Three Stooges movie, yet no one was laughing.

It was a bizarre scene. Couples, families, and business travelers stared, whispered, and pointed fingers at these ugly Americans. Most knew that the obnoxious couple was part of the Beach Boys tour.

Word spread quickly through our entourage that Dennis' wife was outraged because he stashed heroin in his underwear and smuggled it onto our international flight. She discovered his blatantly illegal act during the flight, managed to miraculously relieve Dennis of the contraband (not without causing a scene), and wisely flushed it down the airplane toilet. Dennis' wife wasn't a reckless drug addict like he was, and she'd exercised prudent discretion. That was the full extent of her discretion, though—her temper had no bounds.

Every person on the tour was embarrassed by the spectacle, and we could not distance ourselves fast enough from Dennis and his wife. It was painful to watch; our entire planeload waited to collect our luggage, positioned at the opposite end of the luggage carousel and as far away from the dysfunctional couple as possible. Still, no one could resist watching the train wreck.

Though Brian was as mortified as the rest of us, he tossed off an offhanded zinger, "Maybe we should have checked those two as excess baggage." Everyone within earshot started laughing; Brian could be off-the-charts funny with his clever comments.

Right then I happened to glance over at Mike; the expression on his face was a mixture of sadness and scorn as he watched his cousin Dennis and his wife embarrass everyone associated with the Beach Boys. Mike's look reminded me of our first intimate conversation a year or so before. We were in the back of a tour plane, headed to some forgettable concert, probably in the Midwest, when I surprised myself by asking, "Did you ever drink, Mike?"

"Like a fish."

"What did you drink?"

"Everything! Scotch, vodka, gin, bourbon, tequila, wine. You name it, I drank it. And that's not all I tried. But one day I

Mike Love, the consummate entertainer, balances masterfully on a piano stool. I asked his brother, Steve, for a quote about Mike, and he responded thoughtfully (despite years of estrangement), "Mike never did a bad show. He's still rocking it to this very day, still in there with the likes of fellow music legends Mick Jagger, Bob Dylan, and Paul McCartney."

*Photo by Stan Love
from the Larry Salisbury Collection*

took a good look at Dennis and said to myself, 'I don't want to be like Dennis.' So, I reached down deep inside and pulled back from the edge of self-indulgence, and I chose meditation over self-destruction. I chose a more spiritual path—not a path of perfection, but a more spiritual connection in life. Meditation saved my life."

As I spent more time with the band, I realized Mike's meditation probably also saved the Beach Boys from extinction.

I recognized his sincerity as well as his inner strength, and I know it takes exceptional moral fortitude to overcome one's own vices. During my years with the Beach Boys, I heard Mike say several times that he was addicted to meditation; for that addiction the music world can give thanks.

All of us claimed our luggage as quickly as we could, and we left Dennis standing at the carousel with both arms full of brown paper grocery bags stuffed with his clothes. He had hocked his expensive Louis Vuitton luggage for—yes, you guessed it!—the drugs he smuggled on board.

As soon as Dennis' wife snatched up her luggage, she whirled around and caught the next flight back to Los Angeles. Dennis made it to the curb with his brown paper bags, searching for his limousine, fuming, and complaining loudly, "Where is my fucking limo?" Stan had sent it away, telling the driver that they had overbooked, and tipping him fifty bucks for his trouble. Dennis was forced to spend his last twenty bucks on a cab to take him to the hotel.

While the Dennis-and-wife show was ugly and humiliating, we were all damn lucky. Dennis' smuggling attempt could have become a horrendous international scandal and a disastrous blow to the Beach Boys' comeback.

Our first concert had a poor start, mainly because a drunk

Dennis fell off his drum stool and had to be carried offstage. He was replaced by our back-up drummer, Mike Kowalski, who'd traveled with the band for years and drummed on many recordings. Mike resembled Dennis, had the same lean build, and he was a helluva better drummer. This wasn't the first time he'd bailed out the Beach Boys when Dennis let them down.

When the group departed for Christchurch the next morning, everyone made the flight except Dennis. He chronically missed flights because he overslept after tying one on. It was too much of a pain to deal with him and his hangovers, and that morning *nobody* wanted to wake him up. He was sure to cause a scene and badger the roadies mercilessly for carrying him offstage, insisting that he wasn't drunk and threatening to fire them all. To Dennis, denial was a river in Africa somewhere.

When Dennis finally arrived at the hotel in Christchurch, he needed cash to pay his taxi driver. Staggering drunk, he managed to make it to the front desk and belligerently demanded money. The desk personnel called one of the tour assistants, who quickly showed up and politely apologized to the hotel management. The production team had a big investment in the tour and would do whatever was needed to smooth things over.

After the assistant paid the driver, got Dennis checked in, and escorted him to the elevator, Dennis gave him the slip, saying he needed to find a bathroom right away. Instead, Dennis headed directly to the hotel bar where he knew he could sign for his drinks with his room key.

As soon as he was seated at a table in the lounge with a drink and his brown paper luggage, Dennis began to rant and rave. He appeared to be talking to the paper bags as they perched unresponsively in adjacent chairs, berating them for abandoning him in Auckland. His loud rant annoyed nearby hotel guests, and in less than thirty minutes, he'd cleared out the lounge. Management showed up and asked him to leave the bar, which infuriated Dennis even more. He was loud, disruptive, and obstreperous, sneering, "Do *you* know who *I* am? *I'm* one of the *Beach Boys*! And I'll *buy* this fucking hotel and *fire* all your asses!"

He turned to the unfortunate manager and demanded, "What's your name, asshole?"

Stan and I happened to walk by just then. I was truly shocked. This handsome sex symbol was smashed on his ass at 1:00 p.m. in the afternoon. I turned to Stan. "*Damn*, Dennis is pathetic. I'd even say it's close to tragic, Stan."

Stan was beyond being shocked. "Do you know how many times this same scenario has been played out, everywhere he goes? Dozens. Let's split before he sees us and starts spewing his venomous crap at us."

"Yeah, we should probably get back to the suite in case Dennis decides to pay Brian a visit."

"No worries, bro, I changed Brian's name to an alias. He's now Fred Flintstone. Dennis surely isn't going to come visit you or me. Besides, we're in rooms on both sides of Brian's suite with the adjoining door open so we can see everything at all times."

We made the flight from New Zealand to Australia with no major problems, and the five Brisbane shows went well.

One morning, Brian woke up uncharacteristically early and slipped out of the room. After we discovered he was missing, Stan and I decided to check the delis and snack shops as well as the bar. We were relieved to see Brian in his light-blue Adidas jump suit sitting in the back of the hotel deli, the first place we checked, finishing up a steak sandwich.

When the waitress brought his check, Stan asked, "How do

you plan to pay for your breakfast? You don't have money, and you don't even have a room key."

"I was just gonna tell her I was with the Beach Boys," Brian said innocently. It turns out Brian had eaten two steak sandwiches. It was a damn good thing we showed up in time to pay the bill.

We had no show on our first night in Melbourne; it was slated for the next night. But *no* night is a night off for Brian's personal staff, especially with Dennis around.

Dennis decided he wanted to throw a dinner party, with Brian as his guest of honor. It was mainly a transparent ploy to stick Brian with the check, and it wasn't the first time Dennis had pulled this trick. Brian, being a softy, always fell for it. He didn't know how to say no.

The other guests were the same roadies who'd neglected to collect Dennis back in Auckland. It's a sad scenario when you consider that these were his only friends.

Dennis was famous for ordering multiple bottles of Chateau Lafite Rothschild for the roadies at $300 a pop—this rarified wine for guys who didn't know the difference between Lafite and Laripple.

For his Melbourne dinner party, Dennis insisted that someone other than Stan or I be Brian's sole protector, ostensibly because the table of twelve was full. The truth was simply that Honest Injun was easy to manipulate.

Stephen sensed a potential train wreck waiting to happen, and he vehemently objected to Dennis' ridiculous stipulation. Unfortunately, Dennis persuaded the famously silver-tongued David Frost to call Stephen and pressure him.

Frost could be extremely persuasive and downright demanding. He promised that Dennis wouldn't be a threat to

Brian; his assistant had verified that Dennis did not have any cash.

Stephen didn't wish to alienate Frost, who was a powerful figure and budding concert promoter. Against his own better judgment, Stephen reluctantly agreed once Frost personally guaranteed that Dennis' dinner party would take place in the hotel restaurant. Stephen had a gnawing, deep-down bad feeling about this dinner, and so did Stan and I. At least it would take place where we could keep an eye on things, we reassured ourselves.

That evening at 8:00 sharp, Stan and I sat in the hotel lounge and watched the motley crew file into the elegant restaurant: Dennis, Brian, Honest Injun, and nine somewhat scruffy roadies. When Dennis spotted us, he stopped the guys, huddled them up, and whispered something. They burst into raucous laughter, and as a group, they turned around and flipped us the finger—everyone except Brian.

Stan nudged me, hissing, "Honest Injun's days are numbered."

"He actually flipped us off, that little fat fuck!"

"At least *Brian* had a little respect," Stan said in his cousin's defense.

Two minutes later, we ducked into the restaurant to check on the misfits, and the maître d' pointed out where they were seated in a private banquet room in the back of the restaurant, near the kitchen. We could barely catch a glimpse of Dennis at the head of the table.

Satisfied for the time being, we asked to be seated where we could keep an eye on Brian. Though there wasn't a table with a direct view into the private room, we were seated at the closest table. We placed our dinner orders as two waiters carried trays with a dozen or so cocktails and beers to the rear of the restaurant. I waved at the drinks, and said, "I assume those are for Dennis' diplomats."

Stan and I received our salads a few minutes later; we still held out hope for an uneventful evening. Before we dug into our salads, Stan said he was going to do a quick check on the guys. He walked to the private room's open door, whirled, and rushed back, a horrified look on his face. "They're *gone!*"

"*What?* You're kidding!" I couldn't believe it.

"No, they had to have gone out through the kitchen." We bolted into the kitchen, and Stan shouted: "Did a bunch of guys just come through here?"

One of the waiters we'd seen with the cocktails said, "Yes, they went out the rear door. One guy gave me a hundred bucks for the drinks and told me to keep my mouth shut."

We ran to the rear door and looked out into an empty service alley. It led to a busy city street, bustling with taxis.

"They had to have grabbed taxis. They're gone!" Stan exclaimed in exasperation.

"Oh, shit, so what do you want to do?"

"Let's go tell Stephen."

As we left the restaurant, Stan gave the maître d' sixty bucks and asked him to have our dinners wrapped up, saying we'd be back. We rushed up to Stephen's room and pounded on the door. He answered, looking anxious.

"They split," Stan said.

"*What?* You gotta be kidding me. How the *hell* did they do that?"

"They slipped out through the kitchen. We had the closest table to the banquet room, but it didn't have a clear view of the entry to the kitchen. We saw the waiters taking drinks to them when we were seated. Less than five minutes later, I walked over to look in on them and noticed I couldn't see Dennis sitting at the head of the table, so I rushed into the room and sure enough, their cocktail glasses and beer bottles were empty, and they were gone. We dashed into the kitchen, and the waiter told us that the whole group went out the back door. He got a hundred bucks for the drinks and was told to keep his mouth shut. The kitchen door leads right to the street about fifty feet away. It probably didn't take them more than thirty seconds to hustle through the kitchen and jam to the street where there are taxis everywhere."

"Oh, *damn*. This is all we needed," Stephen growled.

For once, I was the calmest guy in the room. "Listen, let's not get carried away. Right now, all we know is Dennis is up to his lame tricks. Giving us the slip is just a big game to him. You know, like he's in a mystery movie, and he just gave the cops the slip."

Stan cut in, "Yeah, a mystery movie running in his own mind, only he's the one who doesn't have a clue."

"Just the same, right now they're probably just at a different restaurant and Dennis is feeling like Butch Cassidy. We have no evidence drugs are in play." I hoped I was right.

"*Yet.*" Stephen fumed.

"True, but let's just keep cool."

Just then the doorbell rang; Stephen's room service arrived. "Shit, I just lost my appetite."

"Speaking of which," I added, "Stan, why don't you kick back with Stephen and I'll get our to-go dinners, okay? I'll be back in a flash."

I returned in a few minutes. "Hey, maybe Honest Injun will have enough sense to call you, Stephen. You know, so he won't get fired."

"Oh, he's going to get fired all right—for going along with Dennis' bullshit." Examining our options and fretting over this turn of events, Stephen summed up, "All right, Brian doesn't have money on him. Dennis shouldn't have any money. Some of these guys may be dumb enough to go along with this caper, but none of them would be dumb enough to give Brian money, would they?"

After a brief hesitation, Stan and I agreed it was unlikely.

Stan added, "They're dumb enough to go along with dinner but most likely not with the money thing. "

Stephen was certain they'd listen to him. "I warned every single one of them before leaving on this tour that if they gave Brian or Dennis any money for any reason, they would on no uncertain terms be fired."

"Well, *someone* gave the waiter a hundred dollars," Stan snapped.

"Yeah, but technically it wasn't given to Brian or Dennis. Someone just paid for a round of drinks," Stephen pointed out.

"I'm going to lose it if Brian gets drugs tonight," Stan said tightly.

"All right, maybe you guys should wait in Brian's suite in case Honest Injun calls there. Or maybe he'll come to his senses and call me here."

Stan grunted, "What senses? Stephen, you sure as hell better fire him for this or I'm going to kick his ass all the way back to California."

I added fuel to the fire. "He did flip us off with the rest of them."

"*What's* that?" Stephen wasn't sure he had heard me right.

"Dennis saw us in the lounge area when his motley crew was gathering together. Before they went into the restaurant,

Dennis huddled them up and then they all turned around and flipped us off, including that dumb fuck, and at least *he* is supposed to be on our team. He's *not* on our team, Stephen."

Stephen stood up. "That's going to cost him a thousand bucks even if drugs don't come into play, and *then* I'm going to fire his ass. If I had been there when he did that, he'd be on a plane right now."

I wondered aloud, "You don't think Carl would give Dennis any money, do you?"

Stephen pondered that possibility. "Carl may be the youngest Wilson brother, but he's also the group leader. I can't imagine he would be that foolish. I called him personally and made him give me his word that he wouldn't give Dennis any money."

Stan was not convinced. "Yeah, well, *I* can! I can definitely imagine it. I can see Dennis going right up to Carl and asking him for money and, if Carl says no, grabbing him, taking his wallet, and helping himself to Carl's cash. Carl's a pussy. Dennis is still Carl's older brother, and even though he's small, he's a bully. He's a streetwise, rat-packing lowlife. I can only imagine how many dudes he and his degenerate Venice buddies have jumped, beaten, and robbed. You know how many times I've heard Dennis bragging about shit like that, with that crazed, sick, Charles Manson look in his eyes?

"Not only did Dennis' dad beat him up practically every day of his teenage life, but Dennis was a regular menace to the neighborhood."

"Jesus, don't sugar coat it, Stan," Stephen laughed despite himself.

I added, "I have to admit, I think what Dennis gets off on, more than anything else, is scaring people. When he's drinking he's like a sociopath. Add drugs to the equation, and *voilà*, you've got a monster on your hands."

"You guys sure paint a pretty picture," Stephen deadpanned. "So much for not worrying."

"Sorry, Stephen, but let's face it. The three of us are gonna stress to the max until Brian's back." Undiplomatically, I added, "And your 'Brian's Back' slogan is even more appropriate now."

Stan picked up on that, and said, "Let's just hope Brian gets back all in one piece or somebody's going home in a body bag."

"Screw that," I said. "Let's just throw him off a balcony."

Stephen shrugged. "Ok, listen up. Why don't you guys check around at some of the nearby restaurants and see if you can find them? I'm going to notify the tour sponsor that we have a situation on our hands."

As Stan and I headed toward the door, Stan told Stephen, "Good idea, we'll check around some of the other restaurants. Maybe we'll get lucky. Either way, we'll call you every half hour, just to keep you posted. Don't worry, like Rocky said, so far there are no drugs in the mix."

Stephen sighed. "Yeah, well, let's just pray that remains the case."

Chapter Thirteen

Close Call

Stan and I checked every half-way decent restaurant near the hotel and didn't find a trace of Brian or our runaway crew. Worried, we returned to Brian's suite and called Stephen.

Stan demanded, "Any word?"

"Not a peep." Stephen sighed. "Those guys got a lot of nerve pulling a stunt like this and thinking they won't be held accountable. Look, it's almost midnight. There's nothing more we can do. Just hang tight and call me the minute you hear anything. I don't care what time it is. Jesus, we're only halfway into the tour and Brian's missing in action. What a nightmare!"

Stan interrupted Stephen's lament. "Hold on, I think someone's at the door." He put the phone down, and we rushed to the door and pulled it open. Sure enough, the wayward bodyguard was standing at the door, a sheepish look on his face—alone!

Stan whispered, furious, "Where the *fuck* is Brian?"

"He's on his way up."

Stan ran back to the phone, took a deep breath, and nonchalantly said, "Brian's on his way up. Everything is OK.

Call you back."

"Is he all right?"

"Yeah, he's all right." Stan hoped he wasn't lying.

"I'm coming right down!"

"No need, bro. It's fine—he'll be in the room and tucked into bed before you can get down here." He covered the phone, turned to Injun. "You'd better not be making a liar out of me. What the hell do you mean, 'He's on his way up?'"

"He's a little wobbly and a couple of the roadies are helping him."

"Is he drunk?" Stan had steel in his tone. "Did you let him have anything to drink?"

"No, of course not. Just one after-dinner grasshopper is all. You know how he loves those. There's just a little crème de menthe in them."

Stan gritted his teeth. "So, the answer is *yes*. You *did* let him have something to drink. And we don't need you to tell us he loves grasshoppers, or what's in them, do we"

We could all hear Stephen squawking through the earpiece. Stan got back on the phone and tried to calm him down. "Everything's cool, bro. No sense getting yourself any more worked up at this hour. Just relax and get some sleep. We got everything under control."

"I've been worked up all night!"

"So, that's why I'm saying *relax*. We've got this. You can see him in the morning. How's that, all right?" He hung up without waiting for an answer.

"I'm gonna meet the elevator," I said as I ran out of the room. When I stepped out into the hall, I saw two of the larger roadies holding Brian up near the elevators. He was stumbling along, eyes closed, barely able to keep on his feet.

I knew what happened, there were no doubts—Brian was nodding off from some serious drugs, probably heroin. I'd seen the look before. As I rushed down the hall to help, I knew someone was going to pay for this. I'd figure out a way.

We had Brian in the room in seconds, and I checked him out. He was nodding off, all right, but I was sure he was not overdosing. I told the roadies to get the hell out and started to put my plan together as Stan got Brian stretched out on the couch.

Doing my best to sound like the bad cop in an interrogation, I eyed Honest Injun and demanded, "Were you with Brian the whole time?"

"Yes, every minute."

"Did he go to the bathroom?"

"Yeah."

"Did you go with him?"

"Well, no."

"Was he sitting next to Dennis?"

"Yeah."

"Well, there you have it."

"What do you mean?" The dumb shit still didn't get it.

"Dennis slipped him heroin under the table—right under your fucking nose."

His jaw dropped.

"And I'll bet Dennis went to the bathroom right before Brian, didn't he?"

"Come to think of it, uh, yeah—he did."

"After dinner, Dennis went to the bathroom and snorted half of what he was holding, then slipped Brian the other half under the table. Brian then went to the bathroom and snorted the rest of the shit," I theorized.

"But Dennis promised me no drugs," the clueless bodyguard whined.

"And you *believed* him?"

"Well, yeah."

"He's a fucking *drug* addict for Christ's sake—he can't be trusted," I explained, as if talking to a child.

"Why would he lie to me?" he asked, bewildered.

"Why? He's a *drug* addict! Dennis would throw you under the bus for a twenty-dollar bag of smack in a New York minute, any day."

The bodyguard whimpered, "I would never have thought Dennis would do this!"

"You never thought, *period!* And you flipped us off, you little fat fuck. That means you jumped ship. You might just as well have said, '*Fuck you*' to Stan and me. You let Dennis use you, you idiot." I turned my attention to Brian. His eyes were still closed and his head was wobbly—he was definitely nodding off, but he looked okay otherwise. I decided to make this a moment the knucklehead bodyguard would never forget.

I held Brian's face and moved it from side to side. "NASA, we've got a problem. His eyes are rolling back in his head. That means he's overdosing!" I put my acting lessons to good use and sounded the alarm. "Stan, we've got to get Brian in the bathtub and fill it with ice and cold water." I turned to Honest Injun. "We're gonna need all the ice we can get. Go get all you can find—*now!*"

"Why me?"

Stan had heard enough. He spun around and grabbed the so-called bodyguard by the throat, picking him right off his feet, and snarled, "Because he got drugs on *your watch*, asshole!"

"Stan, we don't have time for this bullshit," I interrupted. "Don't kill him yet—we need the ice. Help me get Brian in the bathroom and into the bathtub."

Stan practically threw the bodyguard across the room; he fell hard and scrambled to his feet. He had to be desperate to get away from us, but he couldn't move. He just stood there, scared shitless.

Stan roared, *"Get the ice before I throw your ass off the balcony!"* That unlocked the bodyguard's frozen reflexes and he bolted for the door.

Before he was out of earshot, Stan said, "If Brian doesn't make it, I *am* going to throw that dumb fuck off the balcony, I swear to God."

"I'll help ya."

After the door closed, I began to laugh, quietly. "I'm pretty sure Brian didn't overdose. He's just nodding off."

"Man, Rocky, you could have told me! I really thought he was overdosing and I was totally freaked out, bro. Couldn't you have given me a heads-up?"

"What? And spoil all the fun? I needed to freak you out."

He was speechless, his mouth open, so I continued, "The look on his face when you choked him was priceless. He really thought you were going to throw him off the balcony."

Stan said flatly, "I almost did."

"I would've stopped you before you actually tossed him."

We turned our attention back to Brian, and Stan and I wrapped our arms around his broad shoulders and got him up and walking around. Within a couple of minutes, he looked as though he was starting to come out of it.

Brian mumbled, "What's going on?"

"We're walking you around because you almost overdosed on heroin, big guy."

"I did what? OD'd? No—I didn't!"

"Yes, you did, Brian. You snorted heroin Dennis gave you, and you were out cold. Don't even try to deny it," I said as evenly as I could. "Listen, Stan, we've got to keep him walking around to keep him from relapsing into a coma. You hear that, Brian?"

"Yeah, you're right, Rocky, we need him walking around," Stan said. "You had us scared to death. You keeled over and couldn't move; your eyes were rolled back up in your head. What's the matter, Brian? You can't even remember the last half hour, can you? That's because you were almost dead! You scared the *shit* out of us!"

"I won't do it again," Brian pleaded.

"Your promises are worthless," Stan said scornfully.

"I swear, never again! Dennis gave me too much."

"Yeah, it's Dennis' fault. You're unbelievable, Brian."

"That stuff's never done me any good," Brian said, lamely. "It's bad news."

"We're freaking out here, Brian. If Stan and I hadn't been here, you might be dead!"

"I think I have to pee," Brian said.

"Perfect timing. Stan, take him in the bathroom and don't bring him out until I give you the word."

In a few minutes, the bodyguard returned with bags of ice.

"Give me that stuff and get the fuck out of my sight. If I see you again tonight, I'm liable to kick your ass! You'd better hope Brian makes it."

He scurried away.

Stan brought Brian back out for some more walking therapy. After a couple more laps around the suite, we figured it was safe to put Brian to bed.

Early the next morning, Stephen rapped on the door. When we let him in, the first thing out of his mouth was, "Where's Brian?" I opened the door to Brian's room, and Stephen could see he was sleeping like a baby.

We sat Stephen down in the living room, and Stan and I told him everything, leaving nothing out—including the near-overdose.

Stephen had started to turn pale; he gathered himself, and said, "Man, you guys had me going there. But you know, we'll never *really* know how close Brian came to overdosing. We'd kept him clean for a good long time and a small amount could have simply taken him out. You said it was about twenty minutes before he opened his eyes. That couldn't have been a good thing. Either way, that was *way* too close a call. At least one thing's clear—I'm going to fire the guy responsible for him."

"Yeah," I laughed. "I bet he'll prefer that to the way out *we* offered him. It's a long drop from the balcony."

The three of us chuckled.

Stephen said, more seriously, "This puts Dennis in the hot seat, even though we can't technically prove he actually gave Brian the heroin. But everyone will know it. We can insist that Dennis is off limits to Brian from now on, and we definitely have to make sure Brian doesn't get any more drugs."

"He won't get any more drugs, not on *our* watch," Stan said confidently.

I nodded my agreement.

"As far as Marilyn goes," Stephen continued, "I'll talk to her.

I've got to keep her informed of something this serious. I'll tell her I fired the guy responsible; without him around, she'll feel more secure about Brian being on the tour, and she won't feel the need to pull the plug.

"I'll also tell the production company exactly what we're up against with Dennis so we can enlist their full support. We still don't know who gave Dennis the heroin—or who gave Dennis the money to buy it—two extremely important unanswered questions. But one thing we know for sure—Dennis has got to be stopped!"

Chapter Fourteen

The Sound Check

We were determined that the Down Under tour go off without another incident. Imagine the headlines if an ugly international scandal were to unfold: "Beach Boys' Leader Brian Wilson Overdoses on Heroin during Aussie Tour," or "Beach Boys' Drummer Dennis Wilson is Jailed in Sydney for Possession of Heroin" (or, even worse, involuntary manslaughter).

America's Band would not be looking so all-American. We had all dodged a bullet.

Stephen, Stan, and I acknowledged the obvious fact: Brian could never be alone with that so-called bodyguard ever again (that guy was forever out of the picture). Stan and I also realized the job of monitoring Brian just got a hell of a lot tougher. We were the only remaining guys responsible for him, we were in a foreign country without backup for the next three weeks, and Dennis was still on the scene.

The sound check for that night's giant Melbourne concert was scheduled for 1 p.m., and things were going smoothly. We delivered Brian to the venue with no further complications. To keep him from feeling smothered, Stan and I took turns lurking close by with a clear sightline.

It wasn't long before Dennis approached Brian and said, "I need to talk to you in private."

Stan stepped between them and said, "Not on your life. You want a friend? Get a *dog*—and get your sorry ass out of my sight!"

Dennis got the message. We weren't going to let him approach within ten feet of Brian.

The sound check was winding down, and I was seated in the audience enjoying the experience. I never tired of this milieu; I would have loved to be in a successful rock-and-roll band. Who wouldn't?

My fantasy was interrupted by a rugged six-foot, 230-pound rugby-player type I'd seen backstage during the tour. "Are you Rocky?"

"Yeah. What can I do for you?"

"You're on Brian's staff, yes?"

"I am. Who're you?"

"My name is Marvin. I work for the production company down here."

"Okay. What's up?"

Marvin sat down next to me and leaned in so as not to be overheard. My antennae shot up. He whispered, "I need to talk to you about Brian."

"I'm listening."

Marvin cleared his throat, looked behind him, first right and then left. "Brian keeps asking me to . . . um . . . to get him . . . some, uh . . ."

"Spit it out, man."

And in a barely audible voice, Marvin murmured, "Drugs."

"Jesus Christ!" I exploded.

Marvin continued, and he looked sincere. "I told him *no*

way. I swear it, but he keeps asking me and bugging me and pestering me and, frankly, it's driving me crazy, mate. We were all warned about Brian's 'condition' and told that our jobs depended on helping you guys keep him drug-free while he is visiting our country. I don't want to lose my job!"

Reeling from the nightmarish revelation that Brian was trying to score more drugs after what happened last night, I asked, "What kind of drugs?"

After a long hesitation, Marvin tersely said, "Heroin."

"Oh, my God!"

"I keep telling him 'No.' I swear, Rocky."

I thought for a moment, and asked Marvin, "Why *you*?"

"What?"

"Why does he keep asking *you* for drugs?" I persisted.

Marvin stammered, "I . . . uh . . . ah . . . I don't know."

"Listen to me, Marvin, and listen good. I'm going to ask you this one time... and one time only, and your honesty in answering will determine your future. If you lie to me, you'll not only lose your job, but I'll have you handcuffed and dragged out of here. Do you understand me?"

After a long pause, Marvin said, "Yes."

"Did you provide Dennis with heroin last night?"

After an even longer pause Marvin admitted in a very low voice, "I did." Then he blurted, "But I didn't know *Brian* was going to start asking me for some, or I wouldn't have done it. I swear. I asked Dennis, 'Is this just for you?' He said, 'Yeah, don't worry.' He swore to me, man."

"And you believed him?" I asked incredulously. "Do you use heroin?"

"No, never," Marvin said quickly.

"But you provided heroin to a Beach Boy on a major

international tour—and believed the word of a drug addict when he said he wouldn't give any to his brother?"

"But Dennis seemed okay." Marvin added, "I mean, you know, he seemed fairly normal. But I can tell Brian isn't so—you know—normal."

"You're absolutely right, he's not. Brian has permanent brain damage from drugs. And Dennis gave some of his heroin to Brian—who almost died last night! He was slipping into a coma when Stan and I, thank God, got to him. He was overdosing. We had to put him in a bathtub full of ice water, and then walk him around, before he came out of it. Do you realize you could have been charged as an accessory to manslaughter, Marvin? Your life as you know it would be over."

"That's why I'm coming to you, "Marvin said contritely. "I feel terrible. I'm truly sorry."

Through my outrage, I could see the sincerity in Marvin's eyes, and I felt compassion for the poor guy. He was just trying to be cool and do a favor for a rock star. Like it was *only* a little heroin!

"All right, listen to me. You did the right thing coming to me. Now I want you to come with me and tell Stephen Love everything you just told me. He's Brian's first cousin and the Beach Boys' manager. He's your only hope. Don't even think about splitting. I'll catch you.

"Stephen's a reasonable person—and nobody wants an international incident. Come with me. In fact, you lead the way. Stephen is the redheaded smart-looking guy standing over there. You've got one opportunity. Make good on it."

I introduced Marvin to Stephen, adding, "This man has something to tell you," and I left them alone. From a distance, I watched Stephen's face turn hot pink, then beet red. I can't

THE SOUNDCHECK

Cousins Brian Wilson (left), Steve Love (center), and Carl Wilson talk backstage at a 1978 concert in Sydney, Australia.

*Photo by Stan Love
from the Larry Salisbury Collection*

swear to it, but smoke may have been coming out of his ears.

Then I left to update Stan. "Brian is absolutely incorrigible. He's seriously trying to get more heroin after nearly overdosing last night. Can you believe it?"

Stan looked like he was going to kill someone. I knew that look well, so I added, "Try not to hurt anyone, Stan, except maybe Dennis, our fucking drug addict lowlife."

Stan assured me, "Oh, he's at the top of my list, believe me. I want to strangle him! How's Stephen reacting?"

"As well as can be expected. He was turning three shades of red when I left and he was fuming. But he'll handle it. He always does. Hey, I'm going back to the hotel with Stephen. I know I don't have to tell you to stick to Brian like glue. See you back at the ranch."

He said, "All right, see ya back at the hotel."

I nodded back, "Later," and rejoined Stephen, who also looked like he wanted to tackle someone. Stephen had warned

Marvin to be available for an emergency meeting right after the show tonight, or he would never work with the Beach Boys again.

Considering that we were halfway into the tour, Marvin would lose a sizeable chunk of income if he were let go. He knew it'd also damage his reputation, making it harder to get gigs, so he gave Stephen his room number and assured him that he'd be available.

As Stephen and I were about to climb into the limo, Al Jardine, the only non-family member of the Beach Boys, approached. He said he wasn't feeling well and asked if he could bum a ride back to the hotel with us.

Stephen said, "Yeah. As a matter of fact, there's something very serious I need to fill you in on." He unloaded everything on Al, who was flabbergasted and stunned.

Stephen had a world of trouble on his mind. After all, Brian's life was at stake here. With the recently departed screwup out of the picture, Stan and I would have to redouble our efforts to keep Brian alive—*and* clean *and* playing music—for the duration of the three-week tour.

Stephen's "Brian's Back" campaign was on the line; the campaign and the responsibility for this very important international tour were squarely on his shoulders. The only way to safeguard and preserve the integrity of the public relations campaign and keep the profitable juggernaut of this record-breaking tour on track was to keep Brian safe. The world had to see that Brian was active and fully functioning in his life and career.

It was imperative that Brian perform—stone-cold sober—at every show on our three-week tour. Here we were—with eight shows under our belts, and seven to go.

Chapter Fifteen

The Showdown

Stephen arranged for the meeting to be held in Mike Love's suite after the concert, since Mike was a strong anti-drug advocate, as was fellow band member Al Jardine. Mike had been just as appalled when he learned about Brian's overdose from Al and Stephen, and they thought this would be the right setting for the showdown.

Before Stan and I showed up, representatives from the tour promotors had already filed in and seated themselves, including Marvin's boss and the very British and verbose David Frost. The Beach Boys were represented by Stephen Love, Mike Love, Carl Wilson, and Steve Arnett, the band's accountant and Stephen's hand-picked aide. The atmosphere was somber.

Because it was essential that both Stan and I attend the meeting, Stephen arranged for Jason Raphalian, the band's chief roadie and a big strong guy, to watch Brian for the duration. Stephen instructed Jason that Brian was not allowed to step one foot outside of his suite for any reason, under *any* circumstance, other than a fire or earthquake.

Before Stan and I entered the room, he stopped in the hall, opened his new gold Halliburton briefcase, and turned on a small tape recorder. He had bought the recorder before the tour and had it installed inside the metal case, specifically for this trip. When I asked him why he was using this amateur spy mechanism, he said, "I don't really trust any of these guys. I want to cover my ass, just in case."

When we walked into the suite, we had to edge around a serving cart parked just inside the door, loaded with appetizers.

Carl Wilson stood next to the cart, stuffing his face with finger food, trying to prove that he was unintimidated and ready for battle. Everyone else was seated, ignoring the food.

As Stan and I walked by, Carl blurted with a full mouth, "I didn't have nothin' to do with Brian getting sick last night." The guy sitting closest to Carl was sprayed with food, and I watched him pick a chunk of food off his cheek.

I replied acidly, "You mean the heroin Brian got from Dennis? Is that what you had nothing to do with, Carl?"

"I don't know *nothin'* about any heroin."

I snapped back, "Well, Dennis got heroin and gave some to Brian at his dinner party."

Still spitting food, Carl blabbered, "I wasn't at the dinner and you can't prove Dennis gave Brian heroin—I mean—that Dennis had any heroin!"

"Oh, yes we can! Brian admitted that Dennis slipped him some heroin under the table at the end of the dinner party. And Brian said he asked Dennis where he got the money for the heroin—and Dennis said you gave him the money." I was winging it, but I felt pretty confident about the facts.

"That's bullshit. Brian would never admit to that or anything like that," Carl countered.

"Yes, he did. He admitted it to me," Stan said, backing me up.

Stephen threw in his support from across the room, "That's right, Carl."

The Showdown

Looking desperate, Carl blurted out, "You guys are full of shit. You can't prove nothin'!"

I raised my voice and said, "No, *you're* full of *finger food*. We know you gave Dennis the hundred dollars he bought the heroin with!"

"You're crazy, Rocky. The truth is, you can't prove a thing, fuckhole," Carl muttered not-so-quietly under his breath as he turned and walked away.

I was about to go ballistic. I turned to Stan. "*What* did he call me? Did he just call me *fuckhole*?"

Stan sensed my rage. Fearful that I was going to wale on Carl right then and there, Stan put his arm around my shoulders and diverted me from my path. He steered me over toward Stephen, who motioned for me to sit next to him.

"I need you to stay cool, Rocky," Stephen said. "You're the quarterback. You got it. I'll be cool—for now."

I reached over, casually picked up the phone, and said, loudly enough for everyone to hear, "Stephen, what's the heroin dealer's room number? You know, Marvin, the guy who came to me today at the sound check and told me—and then you—that he sold heroin to Dennis last night. Wasn't he supposed to be here at this meeting?"

Stephen said, "Yes, Marvin was definitely supposed to be here at this meeting tonight. Room 667."

Nobody spoke. Carl froze in his tracks; he even stopped chewing.

I dialed Marvin's room number and let it ring six times. To my surprise, there was no answer. I looked right at Marvin's boss, who looked away. He turned his gaze on David Frost, who looked down at his watch, avoided eye contact with me, and started to swing his crossed leg.

I hung up, dialed the front desk, and asked if Room 667 was still occupied. After a long pause, the desk clerk told me that the guest in question had just checked out.

"Well, well, well," I said to the clerk, looking over at Frost. "You say, Marvin *just* checked out? How convenient. Did he leave a forwarding number?"

"No."

"Do you have his home address—where I can have a subpoena sent to him?" There was a pause, and then I repeated the desk clerk's words for the benefit of those in our meeting. "You say it seems to have disappeared from your records? And you say that is highly irregular? Would you please inform his employer that Marvin is wanted in connection with the trafficking of heroin?"

After that parting shot, I hung up. Everyone in the room held his breath. The room was thick with tension.

"What a strange coincidence," Stan said.

"There *are* no coincidences," Stephen corrected.

I stood up; everyone froze. I gave Frost and Marvin's boss a withering look, and said loudly, "When you guys get through jerking each other off . . ." I walked over to the service cart as I refocused my glare onto Carl, and continued, "Carl and I will conclude our little unfinished business."

Carl made his second mistake. In a low voice, he grunted, "Asshole!"

"That's *exactly* the business I'm going to finish with you." I helped myself to some fruit and slowly walked back to my seat as I glared at Carl.

David Frost cleared his throat and began speaking in his upper-crust effeminate voice, which made me roll my eyes.

"First off, I thought the show was terrific and I was as

THE SHOWDOWN

ecstatic as everyone else in the audience. It was a breathtaking experience. The only two points I wanted to make are that we're in the middle of a glorious tour that's on the verge of being the most successful tour in Australia ever, record-breaking, a stunning success, due to all of you. The realities of the situation are that the fees that we pay are the result of the backing of one of the biggest financing company in Australia, and we would prefer that they not know of any problems that are going on.

"Obviously, they've got two billion in assets; they might sue us. They would certainly sue *you* for fifty million dollars, because if anything goes wrong... what I'm really saying is that without wishing to interfere in any way, we have a kamikaze pact. *Please* delay any explosions until the tour is over because otherwise our backer would just go berserk. If Dennis left the tour, all hell would break loose, on our heads too."

"This is a veiled threat," Stephen said. "You're threatening us with a potential lawsuit of fifty million dollars if we send a drummer home for buying heroin."

Mike interrupted, "We're not the goddamn Rolling Stones and we don't condone this fucking bullshit, *goddamn* it!"

Stephen nodded to Mike and turned to David Frost. "Mr. Frost."

Frost said in his smarmy way, "Please, Stephen, call me David."

"*Mr.* Frost, *my* main concern is not this glorious tour. *My* main concern is Brian Wilson's mental and physical welfare. And let me make myself perfectly clear—I do not condone drugs—and, particularly, highly dangerous and lethal heroin."

Startled by this comment, Frost tried to regain his poise and said, "Well, I... um ... a ... of *course* you don't. Neither do I. None of us condone its use. We absolutely frown on drug usage of any sort."

Stephen interrupted, "Then what, Mr. Frost, do you propose to do about the heroin that one of the Australian crew admitted procuring and providing to Dennis, besides to sweep it under the rug, which is what I sense you are trying to do?"

Frost looked like he had just been slapped in the face. Practically choking on his words, he cleared his throat and started stammering, "Well, I, I, uh, um, we're just going to have to let everyone slide."

I gritted my teeth. "Slide? I'd be worried about a lawsuit." I raised my voice and yelled at Carl, "Admit *you* bought that crap!"

Carl denied giving drugs to Dennis or Brian. "You know what happened? I flushed it down the toilet. I didn't buy Brian shit or spend a penny on shit."

I yelled, "Then you didn't flush it soon enough!"

"Okay," Carl said. "It's a possibility I was drunk and gave him one hundred dollars, but I really don't think I did."

I was furious. "I thought you didn't know *anything* about any heroin, Carl."

Frost ignored me. "And one hundred percent went down the toilet?"

"Yeah! I watched it go down the drain. I remember because it was one of those black Dalton toilets." Carl was determined to stonewall us.

Frost said, "Let's stop the insults and look at the future for a minute. The point is that to try and send Dennis home causes problems. I think he should have one more chance. I think that your moral stance is absolutely correct, but I think that this tour should not be destroyed because it would be the destruction of the Beach Boys. All I would say is, give him one last chance because the consequences of not doing so are awful."

Mike Love jumped on this with both feet. "Dennis is *not* the kind of person who you can *give* a second chance, He's *not* the kind of person who is trustworthy. What we're considering is sending Dennis home while the rest of us finish the tour. People who like drugs lie, they're *not* trustworthy. I can dig it because I have an addictive personality, but I'm addicted to TM and I meditate my ass off."

Carl interrupted, "Mike, I was addicted to cocaine psychologically for many months last year and I know all about that. I was a fucking wreck. I was terrified because I thought Dennis was going through withdrawal." He paused. There was a long silence. I could hardly believe what I was hearing.

Frost reiterated, "We're just going to have to let everybody slide." He continued to bluster, blubber, and filibuster for an ungodly length of time in his pompous way, all hyperbole and grandiosity. He did his best to cajole, manipulate, deceive, subvert, accuse, and flatter. He was a glib one. No wonder Richard Nixon caved during their famous interview.

Stan was getting all of Frost's long-winded display of grandiloquence on tape. As much as Stephen earnestly and politely tried to appeal to Frost's sense of decency, explaining that Brian's welfare was his number one priority, not the "glorious" tour, not the record-breaking success, and certainly not the money, Frost just could not or would not get it.

I couldn't believe my ears. Frost was nothing but an opportunist—and the biggest blowhard windbag I had ever met. When I couldn't take any more of the bullshit I was hearing, I interrupted. Thank God, I'm at my most eloquent when I'm mad.

"Frost, you asked if you could come in here and talk to us for a few minutes, and all you've done for the last ninety minutes is tell us what we can and can't do. My job is to keep drugs out of Brian's life, nothing more, nothing less. That's what Stephen hired me to do, and that's what Brian's wife Marilyn pays Stan and me to do.

"Make no mistake—Stephen, Stan, and I take this responsibility very seriously. To us this is as serious as a heart attack—or an overdose, if you prefer. Which is exactly what Brian had last night. He was almost out cold when he got back last night with his so-called protector, the guy you insisted be his only bodyguard at Dennis' dinner. This same bungling fool quit and flew back to LA last night after allowing this drug fiasco to occur.

"That happened thanks to you, David. We would never have left Brian alone with that guy if you hadn't insisted.

Stan and I had to put Brian in a bathtub full of ice, all the while praying he wouldn't slip further into a coma.

"Marvin gave Dennis heroin last night, and Dennis gave it to Brian, and it created a dire life and death situation: Brian came within a half inch of dying. Think of that, David. One of the world's greatest singer-songwriters almost OD'd in Australia—on your watch!

"Neither you nor Dennis or Carl or anyone else is going to whitewash this incident and sweep it under the rug. It's not gonna happen. If we have to, Stan and I will get on a plane right now with Brian and go back home, where we don't have people around him who don't give a shit if Brian gets heroin. Oh—and almost *dies!*"

I twisted around to look at Carl, "And make no mistake, Carl, Marvin told Stephen and me today that Dennis got the hundred dollars for the heroin from you. That's right—*you*, Carl!"

The Showdown

Carl belched as he walked over to where Frost was seated, directly across from Stephen, Mike, and me. "That's a lie. You can't prove that. Besides, Marvin's not even here. He's gone. So, don't talk to *me*, Rocky. Talk to someone else. *Fuck* you!"

"Fuck *me*, huh?" I had taken enough of his shit. I leaped out of my chair, hurled myself at Carl, and smashed him in the face. The sound of my fist on his face was a loud, satisfying thud.

The blow knocked Carl out, and he fell to the ground like the sack of shit I contemptuously thought him to be. There was a collective gasp from everyone in the room. I stood over Carl, and said in a firm, controlled voice, "Don't *ever* say 'fuck you' to me."

The room was stunned into silence for ten full seconds while everyone stared down at Carl's still body, wondering if he were dead or alive. He came to, flat on his back, holding the left side of his pudgy face, and moaning.

Several more moments elapsed before anyone spoke. And lo and behold, whom do you think, dear reader, did so first? Why, it was the windbag himself, David Frost. He said to me, "I think you owe Carl a vast apology." Warming to his theme and giving it the full upper crust British accent that he was so famous for, he added with indignation, "You, sir, are a bully."

I stared down at Frost. "I don't care what you think of me, you pompous windbag! And that's the nicest thing I can say about you." I picked up the phone again and threatened, "Why don't I call Brian's wife, Marilyn, right now, and ask her what she thinks about Brian getting heroin that your employee provided. Maybe you can convince her that the heroin Brian got is no big deal, but you'll never convince Stephen, Stan, or *me* it's no big deal."

Waving the phone at him, I asked, "Shall I call Brian's wife for you, David?"

Frost looked stricken and said absolutely nothing for a few seconds. Considering he's the biggest blowhard on either side of the pond, it was particularly satisfying. He recovered quickly, though, and sneered, "Don't talk to me in that manner, Rocky."

I snapped back, "I'll talk to you any way I want. You just want to sweep the whole damn heroin problem under the rug, and every person in this room knows it."

I paused, and looked around, giving everyone in the room a chance to jump in, to come to Frost's defense. Not a single person spoke up on his behalf. I vented one last time. "Brian's life is worth a million of your grand British bullshit words."

No one made any attempt to rebut me. Three people from the production team lifted Carl to his feet, helped him out of the room, and left. I turned to Stephen and joked, "So, hey, capitán, is this meeting adjourned?"

Stephen shook my hand and said, "Yes, it is, Rocky. You have retired the culprit—one of them at least. We'll deal with Dennis soon enough."

At that moment, I felt pretty damn proud of myself, both my words and my actions. At that point in my young life, I seldom worried about the long-reaching consequences of my actions.

Frost, I hate to admit, was right. I did owe Carl an apology. I'd crossed a line when I knocked him out, whether he deserved the humiliation or not. It's the age-old riff between talent and management again; Carl was a Beach Boy, and Stephen worked for the band. Stan and I technically worked for Brian (Marilyn, really), and we were on the bottom rung of the food chain.

The next morning at 10:00 a.m., Stephen got a call from Al Jardine, the current (ever-changing) president of the Beach Boys' organization, requesting his presence at an impromptu

The Showdown

meeting to be held in his suite. Stephen readily agreed to attend the hastily-called get together, fully anticipating some discussion about Dennis and the proper disciplinary action that should be taken. On the way to the meeting, he remembered how just the day before Al had said how appalled he was by the whole heroin incident. He had said it twice, emphatically.

It did strike Stephen as odd, however, that Al hadn't attended the meeting with David Frost. Everyone had been there except Dennis Wilson, the culprit, Marvin, the courier, and Al, the appalled.

When Stephen entered Al's suite, he was very surprised to see an extremely hungover Dennis and a swollen-jawed Carl. The meeting's purpose was made clear up front when Al announced that Stephen must send me home.

Stephen immediately assessed the situation; he understood that Dennis and Carl had intimidated Al or, more accurately, *bullied* him into saying those words. Stephen had the fleeting thought that Dennis had put Al in a headlock and perhaps given him a noogie. He wondered if Carl, all 200-plus pounds of him, sat on little Al until he cried "uncle."

At first a bit shocked at Al's demand, Stephen quickly regained his composure. He walked right up to Al, invading his space, and said flatly, "I am *not* sending Rocky home. Rocky is a hero for having the guts to do what someone should have done a long time ago. Then maybe Brian wouldn't be such a rock-and-roll casualty."

Turning to look over his shoulder at Carl and Dennis, he added, "As for you two boneheaded enablers, why don't you quit trying to kill your brother Brian? After all he's done for you! For once in your lives, quit being part of the problem, and

THE BEACH BOYS' ENDLESS WAVE

Here's Mike Love (left) momentarily turning away from the crowd. He's always comfortable and always totally capable of entertaining a sea of fans. The Beach Boys sold out every concert in Australia and New Zealand during their 1978 Down Under tour, setting attendance records at many venues.

*Photo by Stan Love
from the Larry Salisbury Collection*

try being part of the solution. Heroin is not a game!"

Without another word, Stephen left the room. His loyalty to Stan and me, although admirable, was a management error that would come back to bite him. Carl was not about to forget what he saw as an egregious betrayal.

Yes, sending me home was a horrible idea and would leave Brian vulnerable, but that wasn't the point. Stephen had sided with Stan and me, his "crew," against the band. We could never understand the relationship that the band had built, the bond that they'd strengthened by years of being on the stage together, singing harmony and being adored by their fans. Stephen wasn't in that club, and he never would be. Carl, one

The Showdown

of their own, had been insulted in front of strangers. Someone would pay.

That night, the second Melbourne concert went on, but not without a minor incident. Carl had hired a personal bodyguard for himself. When Stephen, Stan, Brian, and I entered the backstage area, once again Carl was at the hospitality trough, stuffing his bulbous, blimpy ass full of who knows what—cold cuts, chips, dip, candy. He was sporting a massively swollen jaw that made him look like Alvin the Chipmunk.

I walked right up to Carl and laughed, catching his squat bodyguard off-guard (he was busy eating, too). When the unsuspecting Carl turned around, I was within a few inches of his face. Looking down on him, I grinned wolfishly. "We had some fun last night, *didn't* we, Carl?"

Startled, he almost choked on his mouthful of food. Unsure how I suddenly appeared in his face, and worried he might be punched out again, he said absolutely nothing, trying to not provoke me.

While he painfully tried to swallow whatever was in his overstuffed mouth, he glared over at his bodyguard, as if to say, "This is the guy I'm paying you to protect me from, you idiot!" Carl was forced to listen as I repeated, "Yeah, we had some fun, fun, fun last night. Hey, Carl, just think, every time you sing 'Fun, Fun, Fun' you'll think of me—and I'll be thinking of *you*, sweetheart."

I continued to taunt him. "Thank Dennis for getting you punched out, not me. And how *is* your jaw? Don't eat too much, you'll break the zipper on your jumpsuit. Are those prison issue, or just your jammies?"

Carl's bodyguard finally came to life, and squeaked, "I think you should—"

I cut him off. "You *think?* He's not paying you to think, buddy, and he's not paying you enough. So just eat your cold cuts and keep your mouth shut." I gave the guy a defiant look, laughed again, turned, and slowly walked off singing, "And we'll have *Fun, Fun, Fun* any time you pay for heroin!"

I thought I had the last word, but then I heard Carl grumbling under his breath, "You haven't heard the end of this, asshole."

Chapter Sixteen

Fame and Fortune

Most people think they want fame and fortune—the more, the merrier; the sooner in life, the better. The Beach Boys became wildly famous when they were teenagers or barely into their twenties, and it affected them all profoundly.

Fame didn't cause all the Beach Boys to become self-destructive. The youngest Wilson brother, Carl, was an excellent guitar player, once named the "Best Guitarist in the Business" by *Beat Magazine*, a singer with an angelic voice, and a gifted songwriter. He sang lead on many Beach Boys hits, and he was the group's harmony counterpoint swing man. Carl had his ups and downs, but comparatively speaking, he was a pretty stable guy. He loved his brothers and cousin, and his intentions were usually benign. He was susceptible to being bullied, which caused him to make some bad alliances and decisions, and his grudge-holding led to some disastrous complications.

Al Jardine is an accomplished guitar player and a fine singer and songwriter in his own right. He, too, has lived a relatively calm life, and he has been a part of the Beach Boys on and off from co-founding the group in 1962 to playing on their 50th anniversary tour in 2012. He always lived clean, stood up against drugs, and shared a meditative life style with Mike Love, his closest associate in the band.

These two Beach Boys didn't add much discord to the group, at least not intentionally nor very often.

We know how badly fame affected Brian, from agoraphobia to world-class drug abuse, but, thank God, he eventually managed to work through these huge issues and come out the other side relatively unscathed.

Mike was the oldest in the band, the hard-working, nondrinking, drug-free backbone of the group, day in, day out, rain or shine. He never could stand Dennis' shaky work ethic nor his massive drug and alcohol use, even before Dennis sank deeply into being a junkie.

What Dennis had going for him was his movie-star-quality good looks. He was a handsome dude, with a mature, grown-up face even when he was a young teenager, a lean yet muscular body, and a fantastic mane of sun-bleached hair.

Dennis quickly became the Beach Boys' sex symbol when he was still in high school. Unfortunately, he dropped out of school in the 10th grade as the band became better known, and he never really grew up. From the first days, he made the most of being a sex symbol—boy, did he get a *lot* of sex. He became famous for doing groupies before and after shows, anywhere and anytime—sometimes even during intermissions.

Dennis was not only the Beach Boys' sex symbol, he was garnering his own fame as an actor. He starred in *Two Lane Blacktop* with singer-songwriter James Taylor, and word was out in the film industry that Dennis was more than just a heartthrob, that he showed promise in a James Dean sort of way.

As a bonus, Dennis brought some authenticity to the group. As the only real surfer, he came up with the inspiration for the name of the group and the initial focus of brother Brian's creativity, and, some of the fans considered him The Beach Boys' sex symbol. Dennis was a fine show drummer, and in music parlance, always played in the middle of the beat, not as easy as it sounds.

Here's a quote from his *New York Times* obituary: "Ricky Fataar, a substitute drummer for the Beach Boys, once described Dennis Wilson's playing: 'He can't roll or do fancy frills, but he can play out a backbeat, which is what their old records are all about.'"

For most of Dennis' adult life, he hung out in Venice, close to the beach, with anyone who'd buy him a drink. He was like the Duke Kahanamoku of Venice beach, but by the early Seventies, he was a drug addict and no longer a surfer.

One night soon after Stan joined the Lakers in 1973, Stephen and Stan went over to their cousin Dennis' drug-infested stomping grounds in Venice, one block up from the beach. Dennis wanted his cousins to take him to the popular Red Onion restaurant in Redondo Beach. Two bouncers were working the door; it was their job to check IDs and enforce the casual but strict dress code. Shoes were an absolute must for any patron. Tank tops were okay, as were shorts, but everyone is familiar with the "No Shoes, No Service" sign. Everyone's seen it, everyone knows it, and everyone complies with it.

Everyone except Dennis. He was barefoot, and he tried waltzing right in as if it was the most natural thing in the world, as if the place was his, and dirty feet were no big deal. After all, he was at a beach, wasn't he?

Dennis was stopped by the shorter of the doormen, who took a quick dislike to the drummer's arrogant display of entitlement. When Dennis pushed, the bouncer shoved back, hard. Dennis was fired up by this aggressive move, and he rushed the bouncer, itching for a fight.

Dennis got more than he bargained for—his life was about to change dramatically.

The second bouncer, a huge, 6' 5" Asian mountain, grabbed Stan from behind and neutralized him so he couldn't join in the fray. Before Stephen could blink, the smaller bouncer brutally karate chopped Dennis in the throat. The Beach Boy dropped like a rock, clutching his throat, in extreme pain, choking and gasping for air.

Stephen's instincts took over, he stepped forward with a lethal left-right-left combination, and he knocked the bouncer out cold. The bigger bouncer howled in pain as Stan's huge paws bent his middle finger back to the point of breaking, and he suddenly released Stan.

The whole violent encounter took less than ten seconds. The Love brothers pulled Dennis to his feet, and the three of them made a quick getaway before the cops came, sure they'd be arrested for assault and battery and disturbing the peace. Dennis would have probably faced a trespassing charge as well.

And that was Stan's and Stephen's big night of hanging out with the colorful Beach Boy drummer.

Later that night, Stephen got a call from his cousin Carl Wilson. Recognizing Carl's distinctive silken voice, Stephen asked, "Hey, Carl, what's up?"

"Dennis told me what a badass you were tonight. I just wanted to tell you how impressed and grateful I am that you stepped in to protect Dennis. He told me that he was reeling from a hard blow to his throat and you knocked the guy out."

"Well, I wasn't going to let that bouncer hurt Denny any more. It all happened so fast, but I did what I thought was right."

"Thank God you were there. You saved the day, cuz, and I wanted to thank you as soon as I heard what happened. Sleep well, Steve. Good night."

When Stephen told me about that night, he also told me that it changed his relationship with Dennis forever.

"Oh, how so?" I asked, curious.

"Denny could be bumptious at times and would be quick to get in someone's face. He would often try to intimidate people with his physicality."

I vividly remembered when Dennis and I were on the tour plane, and how he flashed the bird at me as he swaggered down the aisle and mouthed "Fuck you!" Yes, he sure did try to intimidate.

Stephen continued, "He even tried to intimidate me. We were on the road, somewhere in the Midwest. I was at the airport rental car desk, arranging for five or six cars for the band and the entourage. Carl was standing next to me when a hyped-up, belligerent Dennis came at me and roared menacingly that I was taking too long. He demanded his own car *now*!

"I turned to Carl and growled, 'Get Denny away from me before I have to hurt him.' Carl reacted immediately and moved Dennis so I could conclude my task in peace.

"I was a leading tackler on my high school football team and took six months of private karate lessons from a Korean master, so I was the wrong person for Dennis to be messing with. After he saw me in action at the Red Onion a year later, Dennis never came close to challenging me physically ever again."

The Red Onion fiasco had more serious repercussions. The bouncer's karate chop damaged Dennis' larynx so severely that surgery was not an option. Many top doctors were consulted, and they held out one hope: If Dennis didn't use his vocal chords to talk or sing for six months, and he did absolutely no smoking, drinking alcohol, and especially no cocaine (his favorite drug at the time), there *might* be some improvement. The doctors begged him to make a serious effort to save and restore his voice.

Did Dennis stop talking, stop smoking two packs of Marlboros a day, stop bonging pot day and night, or stop snorting cocaine by the mound? Not for a moment.

And of course, he didn't stop drinking his beloved Myers's rum with Coke or OJ, even for one day. In fact, this was when he escalated his consumption of rum to nonstop drinking from early morning until the wee hours of the night, at which point he would inevitably pass out.

He adhered to this regimen 24/7 and 365 days a year, year after drunken year, until he drowned, drunk and stoned, soon after his 39th birthday. It was tragic and self-destructive. But hey, he was a Beach Boy, and fame had come too soon and too easily to him. He had no impulse control. In his mind, he was invincible.

Sadly, Dennis' voice was not invincible, and for the rest of his life he sang with a guttural, raspy sound. He sounded like a skid row drunk or someone with throat cancer. It was not pretty.

Turns out, the barefoot, millionaire Beach Boy with the raspy voice was his own worst enemy. Fame made him impervious to advice, too. Nobody could tell him anything.

Dennis was movie-star handsome, he was rich and famous, he was a lusted-after sex symbol, and he was once a very fine singer, but things did not end well for him. Sadly, as a result of his volatile temper, he ended up as a raspy-voiced drug casualty.

CHAPTER SEVENTEEN

Celebrate Like There's No Tomorrow

To celebrate our surviving the Down Under tour (and the other Beach Boys' drug-addled misadventures), Marilyn decided to host a dinner party at the very trendy Nick's Fishmarket in Beverly Hills. There would be eleven of us: Marilyn and Brian; Stephen and his girlfriend, Mary; Stan and his date, Carol; and me, with two of my friends and their dates.

Brian, as expected, resisted the idea of leaving the house, but Marilyn insisted he join the party. She was being thoughtful; she didn't want Stan or me to have to stay with Brian and miss the celebration. The plan was for everyone to meet at the mansion for pre-dinner cocktails, then we'd take two limousines for the short ride to the restaurant.

Stephen arrived a little late and without his girlfriend, explaining that he had a splitting headache and didn't feel up to joining the party. When Brian immediately chimed in that he, too, had a headache and wanted to stay at home, Stephen volunteered to stay with Brian so Stan and I could go and have a good time.

Marilyn said she really wished Stephen would reconsider and go with us, but he maintained that his migraine was too severe for him to be festive.

Marilyn tried once more to persuade him, "Stephen, I have something that will make you feel better. Will you take a Valium?"

Stephen said a little stiffly, strait-laced as always, "I have a strong aversion to taking any medication not prescribed by my doctor."

"I have no such aversion! I'll gladly take Stephen's medicine for him," I joked. "It's a tough job, but someone has to do it."

The other dinner guests picked up on this, and they laughingly and unanimously offered to take his medicine as well.

It was one of those silly nonsensical segues that just seem so funny at the time. What a great excuse to get high. The party atmosphere, in combination with drinks, a little Hawaiian pakalolo, and other so-called medicines, has a way of making the trite seem funny.

(This is my cue to disclose that while Stan and I did our best to keep Brian drug-free, we were known to occasionally party in moderation.)

After party favors were consumed, champagne was served, and toasts were made, we piled into the waiting limos and headed for the restaurant. We shouted, "Don't wait up" as we waved goodbye to Stephen and Brian. Our party arrived at the posh Beverly Hills restaurant a fashionable fifteen minutes late.

The Fishmarket's owner, Nick Nicholas, was a handsome 6'5" Greek giant, a personal friend. I had worked for him at his restaurant in Waikiki, Hawaii, as a waiter. I told Nick that though we would only be a party of eight—not the eleven he was expecting—he needn't worry because we would eat, drink, and be merry enough for a dozen people.

Nick said, "Knowing you, Rocky, I have no doubt." He seated us at one of the best and most visible tables at the front of the restaurant where we could be seen by all. What the hell, this was Beverly Hills and we were about to party!

We started off with two bottles of champagne, one of which was compliments of Nick, and one "compliments of Brian," Stan said.

Because I used to work at Nick's, everyone asked me what I recommended. That was easy: "One of everything!" For appetizers, I suggested Crêpes Madagascar, a minced crab dish rolled in a thin crepe and topped with hollandaise sauce; Oysters Rockefeller, baked and topped with spinach and hollandaise; and Clams Casino, topped with bacon and a vinaigrette dressing. Everyone agreed that my recommendations sounded fabulous, and we happily placed orders for all three.

I ordered my favorite chardonnay to accompany the appetizers, and added, "Let's pause for a brief intermission after the appetizers. After all, we're not in a rush. I think it's kind of crass to rush right from one dish to another. My dining philosophy is that the experience should be an occasion for good conversation and taking the time to enjoy one's dinner companions. Besides, I believe that the imbibing of liquid refreshments is just as important as the consumption of food for a thoroughly enjoyable dining experience."

When I climbed off my soapbox, Marilyn raised her champagne flute and toasted me. "Rocky, you kill me."

With perfect timing, Stan added, "I'll drink to that."

My friend Tom threw in, "I'd like to add, having been roommates with Rocky in Hawaii, that one of his favorite sayings is, 'Here's to one-hour dinners turning into three-hour culinary debauches.' Cheers all around!"

We took our time over the appetizers and talked about—what else—music. Marilyn and her sister Diane had their own band, American Spring, and Brian recorded them, sometimes even joining in. We shared our plans with the other guests: Marilyn and Diane had invited me to sing lead on a song called "California Feelin'," and I was tremendously flattered. It's still available on YouTube, with Brian singing on the chorus, and it's included in a clearer mix on one of the Beach Boy albums.

Finally, I asked for the menus. Our waiter, Dusty, a tall, handsome blonde playboy and another good friend, announced, "Before you folks arrived, I made a bet with the other waiters that this is exactly what Rocky would do—wait to order entrées until after a short appetizer intermission, as I call it; which, by the way, is a little something *I* taught Rocky when he worked with us in Hawaii."

I laughed. "That is absolutely true. And I believe *you* said this so-called intermission tradition is what Nick graciously taught *you*."

Nick suddenly appeared at the table, and he said, "Dusty, I'm glad to hear you have passed on some of the refined elements of my fine dining philosophy. Dining out should be a leisurely experience to be savored with friends and loved ones."

"No one could have said it any better, Nick. My sentiments exactly." Turning to my waiter friend, I asked, "So how much did you win, Dusty?"

"Twenty bucks, Rocky." Dusty pulled out a crisp twenty-dollar bill and showed it around. Everyone laughed.

I pulled out a hundred-dollar bill and said, "Well, then, this makes your winnings tonight a hundred and twenty, my friend."

Dusty said, "Thank you, and the next bottle of wine is on me." His generosity elicited cheers all around.

Stan asked, "So, Rocky, what do you recommend for entrées?"

"I think we should let our excellent waiter Dusty do us that honor."

Nick took that as his cue to leave. "You are in good hands."

Without missing a beat, Dusty gave us the menu play-by-play. "Well, the Fishmarket's trademark specialty is our two-and-a-half-pound live Maine lobster. But I'll bet I can guess what Rocky will order—that would be the Abalone Richie, which is, of course, fresh daily. It is pounded on both sides to ensure maximum tenderness, is lightly dusted in flour and sautéed for precisely one and a half minutes on each side, then topped with freshwater bay shrimp and asparagus tips covered in a lemon and butter demi-glace with capers."

"You know me well, Dusty, and you have my order, but please continue."

"On the lighter side, we have a lovely filet of Dover sole Amandine, sautéed in lemon and butter, with garlic mashed potatoes and asparagus spears. We also have an island favorite, fresh mahi mahi Véronique, which is dorado, sautéed in a light sherry cream sauce with white grapes, served with scalloped potatoes and a spinach soufflé. We also have Alaskan king crab legs that are flown in fresh daily, served with drawn butter and French fries. We also feature Norwegian salmon, stuffed with crab, sautéed, poached or broiled, and served with a savory risotto and asparagus spears. Then, finally, there is Nick's special jumbo shrimp scampi on a bed of angel hair pasta with sautéed peppers, mushrooms and artichoke hearts."

Tom was salivating at this point in the presentation, and he said, "I can't take it any longer, my mouth is watering."

Bob, another guest, said, "I can't take it any longer either. If I hear any more, I won't be able to make a decision."

"Thank you, Dusty." I turned to my dinner companions. "There is another alternative, however." Everyone looked at me. "We could just order two of each and have the entrées placed in the middle of the table and share them. The table's certainly big enough and we'll just have Dusty bring us extra plates."

Everyone looked at each other and burst out laughing.

Stan said, "Why not?"

Marilyn said, "It sounds absolutely decadent."

Everyone raised their glass, "We unanimously agree, Rocky."

Dusty brought another bottle of wine. "I've taken the liberty of offering a different wine. I hope it meets with your approval. It's a nice fumé blanc. It's a bit drier than your fuller-bodied chardonnay and goes particularly well with the rich cream sauces." Dusty poured me a taste in a new glass.

"Wow," was my response after tasting it. I offered it to Marilyn to sample. She sipped it and said, "Wow is right. I love it! That's a new one for me. Thank you, Dusty."

Dusty placed fresh glasses all around for everyone and poured. As we all lifted our glasses, I said in admiration, "Here's to Dusty. Please bring us another bottle of the fumé blanc and pour yourself a glass."

Dusty grinned, "I thought you'd never ask." Once again, Nick appeared at the table. He had a bottle of fumé blanc in one hand and two glasses in the other. He handed the bottle to Dusty and said, "I knew you'd like it, I knew you'd order another one—and I *knew* you'd insist on Dusty and me having a glass with you!"

I laughed and began to clap, and the table joined in. Raising my glass, I toasted, "Didn't I tell you this was the greatest restaurant ever? Here's to Nick and his fabulous Fishmarket." The nearby tables joined in the clapping and toasting to Nick and his Fishmarket. In seconds, the entire restaurant was swept up in the celebration, one of those great, spontaneous, happy moments that sparkles when it happens.

I woozily leaned over and said to Marilyn and Stan, "There's just one thing missing—I wish Stephen were here." In unison, Marilyn and Stan chimed in with, "Hear, hear!"

It was a memorable and festive dinner party. In retrospect, I truly wish that both Brian and Stephen had been able to join us. They needed a carefree evening as much—or more—than I did. Things were about to get *much* tougher in Beach Boy world.

Chapter Eighteen

Betrayal

While we party animals were getting more than our fair share of food and drinks and indulging in an overabundance of toasting everything and anything, Stephen was not having fun. Instead, he was full of the angst brought on by betrayal. Betrayal can work a number on your head. It can engender a feeling of guilt, a feeling that you must have done something to deserve what is happening. You may start to second-guess yourself. Doubts arise.

In Stephen's case, he had no cause to feel guilt or self-doubt. He had spent almost a decade establishing countless valuable business relationships, and he had gained the respect and trust of everyone within the industry. He did all that and managed a business entity while he attended to the endless amount of myriad details that go into setting up major tours. Just putting the 40-date international concert tour together, with the very first concert in Russia by an American rock-and-roll band, was a monumental coup.

His multi-million-dollar record deal with CBS Records was a landmark event in the band's career and helped pave the way for their resurgence and longevity.

But in the talent's mind (the band's collective mind),

Stephen was just an employee. His refusal to send me home after I punched Carl was an unforgiveable betrayal and an insult to the whole band. The band members were as loyal to one another as Stephen was to Stan and me, and they were hell-bent on revenge.

Stephen's personal motto, "to thine own self be true," wasn't gonna fly this time. Forget the facts, forget he did what was right to protect Brian—just don't ever forget the impact of a grudge-holding humiliated star who has loyal bandmates.

We merry revelers eventually made our way back to the Bel Air mansion, and Marilyn, Stan, and I said goodbye to our guests in the driveway. When we opened the front door and walked in, we saw Stephen was still awake in the office; he had an unobstructed view of the master bedroom, where Brian was tucked in, asleep for hours. Marilyn insisted that Stephen spend the night, because she wanted us all to have lunch together the next day and continue the celebration.

After Marilyn got up around 10 a.m., Stephen asked us to gather in the office, and he played a message that Carl had left for her on the answering machine: "Marilyn, we're coming over to your house for a Beach Boys' meeting. We're going to have it tomorrow at three."

"Nice of them to tell me," she said. "I wonder what that's all about?"

Stephen took a deep breath. "I got a call from the guys yesterday. They wanted me to know that I was gonna be fired—again. Dennis, Carl, and Mike make a quorum, and they said, 'Marilyn's vote won't save you.'"

The four of us sat in stunned silence.

Stephen continued, "Wait, it gets worse. When the call ended and I hung up the phone, my girlfriend asked me what that was about. She said I looked as white as a ghost. When I told her, you won't believe what she did. Instead of comforting me, she just asked, 'So you're out of the music business? Does this mean you won't be able to get me a recording contract?' Then she got up and walked upstairs. She came down with her two suitcases and just stood there, unable to look at me. I just looked at her in disbelief until I couldn't stomach it any longer and looked away.

"Some twenty or thirty seconds passed and then I heard myself say *'Leave!'*"

Marilyn walked over to Stephen, wrapped her arms around him, and simply held him. We were quiet, barely breathing, as we processed what Stephen had told us.

I tried to inject a little levity into this extremely tense situation. "Hey guys, how about this? I'll wait out back for the guys. And when they get here, I'll just drown a couple of them in the pool. That'll make it an even vote and Stephen can stay."

Just then Brian walked into the office, smiling. "What's with the meeting? Who are we gonna drown, Rocky?"

"The guys decided to fire Stephen again," I said flatly.

Brian's smile faded. "Are they *really* coming over to do that again? Look what happened to us the last time. We lost millions, and we didn't get to play Russia. You know what, I'm gonna tell all four of them that I'll never tour with them again. And you'll be my personal manager, Stephen."

Stephen choked up. "Brian, you overwhelm me. But the Beach Boys must go on. They're *your* creation, and you and The Beach Boys are an American treasure."

Right on time at 3 p.m., Mike, Carl, and Dennis drove up in Mike's yellow Rolls Royce. Brian, Marilyn, Stephen, Stan, and I were sitting around the pool, enjoying a late lunch.

Our visitors were clearly shocked to see Stephen. They weren't expecting a face-to-face confrontation—they were used to someone sending a memo.

Brian yelled out, "Hey, guys, did you bring your swimming trunks?"

Marilyn added, "Yeah, up for a swim?" She didn't sound too friendly.

Taken aback by Marilyn's tone, the three Beach Boys stopped at the gate, while Al Jardine drove up and parked. As he was getting out of his car, he asked, "Are we having a pool party?"

Brian stood up. "Yeah, at the bottom of the pool!"

Al didn't quite know what to make of that, and he scratched his head. "What's going on?"

At this point, an incensed Marilyn rose to her feet and announced, in a decidedly unfriendly tone of voice, "I'll tell you what's going on. The four of you are getting back in your cars and leaving. *Now!*"

Brian muttered in my direction, "Or we could just drown them."

I took Brian's cue and sang, "If everybody had a pool . . . we could drown these fools!" Everyone at the table roared with laughter, and we started singing the Surfin' USA-like refrain, "If everybody had a pool . . . we could drown these fools!"

Dennis, ever the wiseass, tried a zinger, "*We're* the Beach Boys. *We've* been doing without you for years, Brian! You too, Stephen." When that comment fell flat, the Beach Boys retreated, climbed into their cars and took off.

Stephen shook his head sadly. "Dennis has been waiting to say that to me for years, ever since he asked me to be his best man when he was marrying his second wife for the first time. I politely declined, and that seriously ruffled his feathers."

"I never heard that," I gasped. "You're kidding me! You turned down Mr. Hollywood? He was the *man*."

"Look, Dennis had never invited me out for so much as a cup of coffee before. I wasn't falling for his transparent overture. He was trying to play me and get me to open up the corporate checkbook. I wasn't going to let him play me for a fool. I know I risked alienating him and I sensed there might be adverse ramifications down the road. It's all coming home to roost now."

Changing the subject, Stan piped up, "Hey, Rocky, why don't you make us some of your famous mai tais?"

I looked at Marilyn. She smiled. "I'll get a pitcher of ice and glasses. You get the rum and your special ingredients, and we'll mix up a batch."

Marilyn and I soon returned with a pitcher of fresh mai tais, and I poured a full glass for each of us. Brian raised his glass and said, solemnly, "I want to make a toast to my cousin Stephen, the best damn manager the Beach Boys ever had. Here's to you, Stephen. I love you, man!"

Stephen looked at us, touched by our loyalty. "You all overwhelm me. I want to personally thank the four of you for your tremendous show of support. It means the world to me. It's a helluva send-off."

"Hear, hear! Hear, hear! Here's to Stephen," we cheered as we toasted our friend.

Chapter Nineteen

I Love You

When Stephen was fired, it was the beginning of the end for Stan and me. A few months later, Brian abruptly told Marilyn that he was leaving her. He said he was filing for divorce, and he was moving into his own house in Pacific Palisades, practically next-door to the Riviera Country Club.

Marilyn handled herself with remarkable style and humor. She said, lightly, "What? Are you taking up golf, Brian?" After a beat, learned from years of living with Brian's impeccable timing, she asked, "When are you moving?"

"Right now! I just packed a bag. Someone will pick up the rest of my clothes tomorrow. This's all I'm taking." With his crooked smile, Brian looked at Marilyn for a few long seconds, then he simply said, "Bye." He turned, walked over to the garment bag in the corner of the room, threw it over his shoulder, and sauntered out of the house as if he didn't have a care in the world.

I looked at Marilyn. Though she was stunned, she bravely tried to joke, "Hmm. A Beverly Hills divorce. Fast and feelingless."

Brian wanted to live simply. The only furniture he wanted for his new digs, besides a rented recliner, couch, living room table, two sets of bedroom furniture, and a kitchen table with four chairs, was a punching bag. He didn't stint with the bag; he insisted on a big one, almost four feet long and weighing a good 100 pounds. And he wanted it hung from the ceiling in the middle of the living room, a spot with a view of the back yard and swimming pool through the double sliding glass doors. Brian spent much of his time pacing around the pool or punching the heavy bag. This was his daily routine.

Stan and I were still part of his daily routine, too. We scrupulously maintained Brian's regular fitness and sobriety schedule: He hit the gym daily, played basketball, sweated in the Jacuzzi, sauna, and steam room, took multiple showers, and, on Mondays and Fridays, went to see the shrink. On Tuesdays and Thursdays, the routine varied slightly—we drove Brian to the recording studio.

Brian had a longtime good friend who was a regular in the pickup games at the Santa Monica YMCA with us, and he also dropped in at the new house—Dean Torrence of the Jan and Dean duo of surf music fame. Dean was like family, one of the few people who could show up at Brian's house at any time unannounced and get buzzed right in. Dean was a loyal friend who stuck by Brian's side through thick and thin.

A small digression: I recently reached out to Dean for information on songs that Brian wrote with Jan and Dean of surf music fame, and he said, "Brian gave us 'Surf City' maybe half finished, he had lost interest in it. The melody was done but the lyrics were incomplete, so Jan and I finished the lyrics. Jan wrote the arrangement and we cut the track. When it came time to cut the vocals we called Brian to see if he wanted to participate and of course he did. He and Jan doubled the lead, and then Brian and I doubled all the falsetto parts."

I Love You

Dean Torrance of "Jan and Dean" with Dennis Wilson–a couple of pop stars just goofing off. It is interesting to note that Karen Lamm Wilson, who took this picture, married and divorced Dennis Wilson, twice!

Photo by Karen Lamm Wilson courtesy of Dean Torrance

Ironically, Surf City was the first surf song to hit the Top 100!

They collaborated on other music, as well. Brian also helped write "Dead Man's Curve" and "Drag City"—both Top 10 hits—and Jan and Dean took Brian's "Catch A Wave" melody and adapted their own lyrics to put together "Sidewalk Surfin." It went both ways; Brian and Dean also sang together, doubling the lead on "Barbara Ann" for the Beach Boys' *The Party Album*.

Once he became a bachelor again, Brian seemed to be as carefree as a bird. Without a maid or kitchen skills, the three of us ate out most of the time. Stan and I, always conscientious of his health, were careful to oversee Brian's diet.

Brian missed his daily access to music, and before long, he rented an upright piano for the living room. To our delight and surprise, he played the piano regularly and began to write songs. One day, Brian asked me to help him with some lyrics to a new song, "It's Like Heaven."

"What's the matter with you, Brian? Are you running out of lyrics?"

Brian looked at me, let out a big belly laugh, and said, "That's it!" Then he jubilantly sang, "What's the matter with you, babe? Don't you know I'll see ya through, babe? What's the *matter* with you, babe? What's the matter with you-oo-oo-oo?" He said I'd helped him with the bridge and credited me as co-songwriter on the silly little song.

That year, Shaun Cassidy ended up recording it on his next album, *Under Wraps*, which sold two million copies. Later, I received a royalty check from BMI for $15,000 for my one-line contribution. My little comment wasn't even intended to be a lyric. This was just another example of Brian's generous nature.

One day, after Brian had been at his new digs for three or four months and his quickie, uncontested divorce was halfway final, the phone rang. Brian answered the phone before Stan could see who it was. While Brian was talking, Stan asked him who was calling. Brian brushed him off, turning his back. "Just a friend."

When Brian got off the phone, he was unusually contemplative, and he spent a while pacing around the pool. Finally, he stopped in his tracks, smiled, and said, "That's it! I'll get 'em to take me to a hospital and get—" His voice trailed off, then he went inside and started pounding the punching bag.

About six the next morning, it was starting to get light and the birds were chirping. Brian slipped into Marilyn's Bel Air bedroom, stopped for a second, and looked around. I'm a very light sleeper; I woke up immediately, hyperalert. What came next seemed like a hallucination.

I Love You

Brian walked over to Marilyn's side of the bed, bent down, and kissed her on the cheek. He said softly, "I love you." He walked over to my side of the bed, bent down and kissed me on the cheek. Brian repeated, "I love you," turned, and calmly walked out of the room.

Marilyn and I looked at each other. I said, "I'd better go talk to him."

My mind was racing. Marilyn and I had grown close, and things evolved naturally after Brian moved out of the house. We were careful to keep our relationship discreet, and we certainly hadn't meant for Brian to know until long after their divorce was a distant memory, for everyone's sake. Brian's reaction was unexpected, but by no means was I reassured that a kiss on the cheek was going to be the end of this.

When I got downstairs, the front door was open, and Brian was outside pacing back and forth. I walked over to him. He looked at me, and said, "It's not *fair!*"

I took a breath. "Is it *fair* how you've been ignoring your wife and kids the last ten years, Brian? You've been absent for a decade."

"You love her," Brian said flatly.

I wasn't sure if this was a question. I hesitated. "Maybe I do."

He didn't respond directly. "Can you take me to get some cigarettes?"

I was stunned that cigarettes were foremost in Brian's mind at a time like this, and I took another deep breath. "Yeah, sure. Let me go get the keys to the Cherokee."

Brian waited outside. In less than two minutes, Marilyn and I came down and got into the Jeep. Brian sat in the front passenger seat, and Marilyn rode in back, directly behind him. I drove to the market on Beverly Glen and back. The entire round trip took less than twenty minutes. Brian didn't come in when we got back to Marilyn's.

I called Stan and told him what had just happened.

Stan said, "Brian slipped out and caught a ride with someone about forty-five minutes ago."

"Well, that explains how he got here, and why. Someone wanted Brian to see us. What kind of a jerk would do that?"

Marilyn could hear both sides of the conversation. She said, sadly, "Doesn't really matter who, does it? The damage is done."

"Maybe this whole thing will blow over," I said to Stan. "Brian rode in the car with Marilyn and me and acted like it was nothing, no big deal. I told you what he said and did, this morning when he first saw us—he kissed us both on the cheek, one at time, and said 'I love you.' If I hadn't been there to see and hear it firsthand, I wouldn't believe it.

"It was even more amazing on the ride back, when Marilyn asked him if he had anything to say to her. He was really casual, and he just said, 'No.' Simple as that. Not another word the entire ride to the store and back again."

Marilyn announced that Brian just climbed into someone's car and left. Stan heard her say, "I hope that guy's bringing him back to you, Stan. If he's not back in a half hour, call the police and tell them Brian's been kidnapped."

"I will," Stan promised.

Stan called back a half hour later and reported, "The guy just dropped Brian off. As he drove off, I yelled, 'You do this again and I'll have you arrested for kidnapping.'"

The next day, I showed up at Brian's place for my regular shift. He was pacing around the pool.

I asked Stan, "How long has he been doing that today?"

I Love You

"Since he chugged down his first cup of coffee."

"Maybe he should switch to decaf. He looks a little agitated."

We went outside to the patio.

I cut to the chase. "Brian, are you mad at me?" He didn't answer.

"Are you speaking to me?" Again, no answer.

I muttered to Stan, "This can't be good, can it?"

Stan thought for a few seconds, and suggested, "Maybe you should lie low for a couple of days and hang out at our place. I'll just stay here with him until we see how this thing shakes out."

As Stan said this, Brian turned, rushed towards the house, and surfer stomped the sliding glass door with his bare foot. It rattled all to hell, but luckily didn't break. Stan quickly trotted over to Brian, put his arm around him, and asked, "What's going on, big guy?" Brian shrugged Stan off and resumed pacing around the pool.

Brian was staring at the water, and I had a pang of worry. In the years that I'd been with him, in all our time in the spa and the pool, I'd never actually seen him swim. I quietly asked Stan, "Can he swim?"

Stan was unsure, too, and he called, "Brian, can you swim?"

Brian ignored him, walking even faster. This not-answering shit began to really worry us. Stan pulled me aside. "Rocky, why don't you jump in your car and drive around the block? I'll see if I can get Brian in my car. I'll tell him I'm going to take him to get something to eat. But we better take him to a hospital to get checked out—just to be safe."

When I pulled up after driving around the block, Stan and Brian were just getting into Stan's car. I parked, slid into the back seat behind Stan, and closed the door with a thud. Brian acted like he didn't even notice, but he knew exactly where he was headed.

We drove in silence for twenty minutes to Brotman Memorial Hospital, a Culver City hospital known for its rehab/psych work. Reluctantly, Stan had Brian admitted. He explained to the intake doctor that he was Brian's first cousin and he was afraid Brian might be a danger to himself. He added, in no uncertain terms, that we would be back for Brian in a couple of days.

When Stan and I drove away from Brotman, he said to me, "Remember when they fired Stephen, I said our days were numbered, that it was just a matter of time? Well, now is that time."

"Why do you think that?" I asked.

"Because Brian wants drugs. And he just figured out a way to get them. He's not really pissed at you. But he's going to tell the doctor you're fucking his wife so he can get the doctor to give him Thorazine and get high as a kite."

Stan added, thoughtfully, "After he got off the phone and was pacing around the pool, he suddenly stopped and said out loud, 'That's it! I'll get them to take me to a hospital and get'—he practically said the word—'drugs.'"

"Oh, shit, but he moved out months ago and filed for divorce. He can't be *that* upset."

"Now he's put two and two together and he's figured out how to get his drugs."

Stan called the hospital twice a week asking for updates on when Brian would be released; he complained that he was getting the runaround. After three full weeks, Stan and I were allowed to see Brian in a small downstairs room with the door open and nurses standing by. A security guy hovered within hearing distance as well.

Brian didn't say much. Stan beat around the bush and asked trivial questions such as, "How's it going, Brian? Are you getting good stuff here?"

I Love You

I finally asked Brian, "So, are you speaking to me, Brian?"

With his usual good timing, Brian tossed out, "Well, *you're* fucking my wife."

Stan said, "I told you he would use that as his excuse with the doctors."

"Aren't you divorcing Marilyn, Brian?" I countered. "Didn't you move out months ago? Is Marilyn your wife, or your *ex*-wife?"

Brian didn't say anything, He just sat there. I could imagine what he was thinking.

I tried one more time, "Brian, you checked out a decade ago. You checked out on the Beach Boys! And you also checked out on your wife and kids. Do you even *remember* the last ten years?"

A nurse stepped up and said, harshly, "Okay, that's enough."

Stan stepped in and challenged her. "What are you talking about? Who are you to say that's enough? We've only been talking for a few minutes. We've been his *full-time* caregivers, so to speak, for three years!"

"That's not all, from what *I* understand," The nurse remarked snidely, looking at me.

"Maybe you don't understand," I snapped. "Brian doesn't *have* a wife. He has an *ex*-wife." I gritted my teeth, trying to stay calm. "Do you, by any chance, understand the difference?"

At this point the security guy intervened. "Is there a problem here?"

In a voice dripping with sarcasm, I said, "Do they teach you to talk like that in security school: 'Is there a problem here?'" I was *way* too macho.

Two more security guards appeared and escorted the three of us back upstairs. Stan broke away from the pack and barged into the doctor's office, where he shouted in frustration, "You promised me *three* weeks ago that you would release my cousin Brian to me, or I wouldn't have checked him in. Now I expect you to honor your promise."

"I'm afraid I can't do that at this time." the doctor said, calmly.

I turned around to look at Brian. "You got your drugs, your precious drugs. Your doctors are your drug dealers now—you should all be proud of yourselves."

Brian had outsmarted us and everyone else, including his doctors. They *were* his drug dealers, and there was nothing we could do to stop them.

I felt like crying. I glanced sideways—Stan *was* crying in full view of the nurses, doctor, and security guards. Tears were pouring down his face.

When Brian saw the tears running down Stan's cheeks, he turned away. He couldn't look at his cousin; he knew how badly Stan was hurt. He could not face the very person who had spent the last three years trying to save his life. Brian turned away in shame, as all drug addicts do when they choose their addiction over life and turn their backs on the people who have helped keep them alive.

Brian shed no tears that day. The drugs took his tears away years before.

Chapter Twenty

No Thanks

Marilyn and I met for dinner right after Stan and I visited Brian at the hospital, and I brought her up to date. I knew Marilyn was in a tough spot. Though Brian had left her, the divorce wasn't final, and her legal situation was cloudy at best. I knew she still loved Brian, and our affair certainly added a complicated layer to an already thorny divorce.

In a way, Marilyn was now as helpless as Stan and I were, and without Stephen around, there were bigger forces at play.

I met with Stan the next morning. We agreed that Marilyn wasn't going to be able to help with the doctors or the lawyers.

Stan changed the subject. "I talked to Brian's lawyer about an hour ago. He told me I could continue to work for Brian, only at half of what I was making the last few years."

"What? Are you kidding me? What did you tell him?"

"What do you *think* I told him?"

"Well, I hope you told him you'd take it. $26,000 a year is better than nothing." *What about me?* went through my mind, but I didn't interrupt the story.

"I told him to kiss my ass. I told him that I wouldn't work for a penny less than I was making, $52,000 a year. Hell no!"

I took a big breath and tried to calm down. "Okay, I know what's important here is that we know what we did, and we know what Stephen did. We know the first few years of drug rehab is the most crucial stage in an addict's recovery, and for the first three straight years of Brian's rehab, we kept drugs out of Brian's life, we kept alcohol out of his life, and we even got him to quit smoking cigarettes. Hell, we got him to lose 100 pounds, which was life-saving all by itself.

"We got him in good shape. We even got Brian writing songs again. And if that isn't enough, we got him touring again, for God's sake! Everybody knows he hates touring. I mean, talk about resurrecting someone from the dead. Can I make this any clearer?"

Stan managed a ghost of a smile.

"You know what, Rocky? You're right. And nobody can take that away from us."

"I know it, you know it, and Stephen knows it. And deep down inside, Brian knows it, too. I mean, come on, Stan, let's be real—Brian's way too smart not to know the truth about who really saved him. Now you tell me—isn't that thanks enough?"

* * *

It's 2018, and I'm looking back at Brian's turnaround with the advantage of hindsight. It's clear that Landy wasn't the one who made the difference in Brian's life.

Landy worked for Brian twice. The first time he lasted six months, until Stephen fired him for outrageously escalating his fees. Landy got back into Brian's life five years later, when Carl realized that Brian was going the way of Elvis.

But then Landy became infamous for taking control of Brian's money and career. Hell, Landy was even forcing Brian to write songs with him. The way he treated Brian led to Landy's losing his professional license to practice psychology in California. "The darkest five years of my life", was how Brian described his time with Landy.

Stephen, Stan, and I know who really saved Brian from drug addiction. With all due respect, we saved Brian from himself.

Section III: 1979 and beyond

Chapter Twenty-One

California Feelin'

Others took over when Brian finally left the hospital, and Stan and I no longer had any responsibility for his care. We were officially out of work.

With no job to tie him down, after a few months Stan decided he and his fiancée couldn't pass up the opportunity to move to Stephen's ranch on the Big Island of Hawaii. He and I kept in touch, talking at least once a week. One day, Stan phoned to say that he'd just spoken with his brother Mike for the first time since Brian was in the hospital.

"He was talking about a recording contract for *you*, Rocky. Mike wanted to know if you would be interested in recording an album. Maybe you'll make a hit record." That was my friend Stan, the eternal optimist.

Recording an album was a lifelong dream of mine, and a *very* alluring one at that. I had been writing songs, and I wanted desperately to try my hand at playing a rock star. I had enough self-awareness to know that I was being seduced by my own desires.

A hundred-thousand-dollar budget was available to record an album at Mike's new recording studio in Santa Barbara. Hardly believing my luck, I took the deal in a heartbeat.

Stan offered to fly in from Hawaii to give me moral support during the initial pre-production meeting; I took him up on his offer and was relieved to have him by my side when we met with his older brother.

I hesitated when Mike asked us, "What kind of sound is Rocky looking for?"

Stan jumped in, "Like those guys, Bad Company."

Mike looked at me and shot back, "Oh, *are* you?"

We both got a chuckle out of that. "Bad Company" represented what Mike felt was good old rock and roll and he supported the idea.

I wish I had stuck with my rock and roll concept, but I didn't. I made some terrible decisions along the way. When I recorded my songs, disco was all the rage, and I was seduced again all too easily—this time into converting my rock and roll songs into disco drivel.

What can I say? I caught the back end of the disco era, and when it died—right around the time my album was mixed down—disco was Do Not Resuscitate. It served me right. There went my shot at playing an early American Idol.

It was a huge disappointment. Mike Love had given me a shot at one of my big dreams and I hadn't made the most of it.

Though my music career was as dead as disco, my acting and modeling careers really started to pick up in 1979. And so did my social life. In fact, it became downright hedonistic. I spent way too much time on the party circuit.

Though the Wilson and Love brothers were no longer a big part of my life, I saw Brian a few times after he moved home with his new caregiver. One of those times was a bit of a heartbreaker for me.

Brian and I both lived in Pacific Palisades, an upscale neigh-

CALIFORNIA FEELIN'

borhood just up Sunset Boulevard from the coast. There's a saying about this part of the greater Los Angeles area that goes, "If you're rich, you live in Santa Monica; if you're a star, you live in Malibu; if you're lucky, you live in Pacific Palisades."

I was shopping in a neighborhood grocery story when I heard a strange monolog coming from the next aisle. The voice sounded familiar, and something made me take a look—to my surprise, it was Brian, wandering around aimlessly. It was good to see him. I approached him, and he recognized me, so I gave him a big smile.

"Hey, Brian, who're you talking to? He looked at me with that vague smile of his. His answer was pure Brian: "Oh, no one!"

We made our way to the checkout, where his caregiver was unloading a fully stocked grocery cart, filled with steaks, full slabs of ribs, whole chickens, dozens of burgers, all Brian's favorite foods. When I looked more carefully, I saw that the checker had already rung up a veritable ocean of what must have been a couple hundred dollars of vodka, scotch, wine, beer, the works. My heart sank.

Stephen, Stan, and I had spent the better part of three years keeping that poison out of Brian's reach, and here, less than three months after we parted company, Brian's house was awash in booze. That sweet soul was being poisoned again, and there was no way I could protect him.

I stood quiet, feeling an enormous disappointment, wished him well, and walked away. Regret that I couldn't help him lingers to this day.

Stan came back to the mainland for a visit in January, 1982, and he was in town on Super Bowl Sunday when I went out on a yacht party with some friends. I gave him a call when we sailed back to the marina that evening, and he said, "I'll stop by. I need your help, anyway—there's someone I want to pay a visit to around midnight."

"Whatever—I'm in."

When Stan got to the yacht, he took me aside and told me he'd found out how badly things had gone downhill for Brian over the last three years.

"Do you remember the woman who used to be Stephen's assistant? She called me about Dennis and Brian. My asshole cousin has been borrowing money from Brian so he can buy cocaine. That's bad enough, but what makes me crazy is that he's *sharing* the shit with Brian. It's getting so bad that Brian had a seizure the last time Dennis gave him cocaine. It could have killed him. Apparently, they can't stop it from Brian's side of things. Dennis' addiction is out of control, Brian is just a sitting duck, and something has to change."

Stan sounded ominous. "Rocky, we *have* to go see Dennis."

"Okay, let's go pay Dennis a visit. We're long overdue. Hell, he never gave us any respect anyway, the little punk. He's had this coming his whole life. Someone should have kicked his punk ass a long time ago. Maybe he wouldn't be so cocky."

Three years hadn't lessened our love and loyalty for Brian, and we would take care of his problem, whether we still worked for him or not. We weren't going to stand idly by while Dennis did his damnedest to undo the work we did—saving Brian's life. Stan and I both took Dennis' actions personally.

Some of my fellow yacht guests overheard our conversation, and as we got up to leave, there was a smattering of applause and some cheers: *Yeah, go get 'em! To hell with Dennis. Long live Brian!*

Stan and I cruised over to Dennis' beachfront pad and cased

the joint. By then, it was after midnight, and Dennis was in the kitchen with half a dozen people, snorting his brains out. As we peeked into the windows at the back of the house, Dennis suddenly said, "We're out of booze. Let's make a run."

He and a few of his party buddies jumped into a van and headed to the nearest liquor store on Venice Boulevard. We followed, keeping our distance. On the way, I said to Stan, "When we get there and Dennis and his motley crew go into the liquor store, maybe I should sort of stumble in, kind of happenstance-like, and try to hook up with Dennis; you know, bullshit my way into his pad to party with him. Then, I'll somehow let you in at the right time."

"Good idea. You're already high as a kite, he might just fall for it."

I tried to do just that. I stumbled into the liquor store and made a big show of surprise when I saw Dennis. "Hey, what's happening, Dennis?"

Dennis growled, "What are *you* doing here?"

"Same as you, bro, partying. Let's have some fun, man!"

Dennis was a bit chilly. He grabbed a quart of Myers's dark rum, orange juice, and cigarettes, got his druggie friends to pay for everything, and they piled back into the van. I tried to jump in with them, but Dennis puts the kibosh on that. "There's not enough room, man." Dennis dove head-first into the side door of the van as it sped away.

Now the real fun began. Stan and I drove back to Dennis' shabby, battered rental beach house. I muttered, "Can you imagine a Beach Boy who has made millions renting a dump like this? He doesn't even own a house after twenty years of easy, big money. He may be the good-looking one, but he's also the dumb ass."

We were prowling around the outside perimeter of the house, and Stan suddenly whispered, "Let's just go right through the front door."

"What?"

"Yeah. We'll just knock on the door. I bet he comes to the door himself. He's paranoid and doesn't want anyone interrupting his cocaine party. When he comes to the door and says, 'Who is it?' I'll kick this rickety-ass door right off its hinges. You charge in and body slam him with the door."

"Sounds good to me."

Sure enough, 6'8" long-legged Stan Love kicked the door into Dennis' face as soon as Dennis asked, "Who is it?"

I rushed in like the pro football running back I once was and jumped on top of the door while Dennis was still pinned underneath on the bare floor. Using his considerable strength, Stan grabbed the door and threw it *and* me halfway across the room. Dennis desperately tried to protect his face with his arms while Stan and I beat him from head to toe.

To keep Dennis' guests at bay, Stan yelled, "Freeze! We're the police!" He grabbed the phone, pushed some buttons, and said loudly, "We have everything under control here."

Dennis' so-called friends backed up against the wall and froze. Not one of them lifted a finger to help him. Druggies. Good while the drugs lasted. Good for nothing else.

I cringe when I think how badly we beat Dennis. I tossed him around like a rag doll, doing some damage to the windows, and Stan was in a frenzy, screaming, *"Leave Brian alone!"*

When Dennis stopped begging for mercy and struggling, we decided he'd had enough. As out of control as we were, we still wanted to make sure Dennis was okay before we left. When I leaned down to touch his still body, Dennis struck like a cobra, aiming his fist at my balls but bouncing off my thigh, thank God. Relieved Dennis was conscious, Stan headed for the door. I decided I needed to say goodbye properly, and I punched Dennis a few more times.

As I pushed him away and headed to the door, I said, "The single most important thing to remember, Dennis, is *leave Brian alone*, or we'll be back."

As I went out through the broken front door frame, I ran right into a cop. Stan must have just missed him. The cop flashed a light on my face. "What's going on? It's been reported that there's a disturbance here."

Before I can think of anything to say, Dennis miraculously appeared and, not wanting his cocaine party exposed or interrupted, defused the situation. He was bleeding, clearly beaten to a pulp, and the cop ask if he wanted to press charges. Dennis mustered some cool. "No, it's just a family affair."

"You sure?" the skeptical policeman asked.

"Yeah, I'm sure."

I was blown away that Dennis was not having me arrested.

The cop left, shaking his head. I split, wondering where the hell Stan was, and found him blinking his headlights in the back alley. As Dennis returned to his precious coke, I thought, *He's really going to need it tonight.*

A few hours later, when the sun came up, Stan woke me and said, "Let's go see Dennis."

"Are you fucking *serious*?"

"Yeah, I'm as serious as a heart attack. And that's exactly what I want Dennis to have, when he sees us at his pad again. I want him to know that we will be back if he ever gives Brian drugs again. You don't think he gets it yet, do ya? He's not gonna leave Brian alone! But when we show back up this morning—

and he probably hasn't even slept yet—he'll get the message."

"Okay, sounds like fun. Let's go. I can't wait to see the expression on his face when his worst nightmare returns."

Back at Dennis' house, Stan and I moved the unhinged wooden door which was leaning drunkenly against the doorframe, and we waltzed in. Dennis was sitting on a small stool, his back against the kitchen wall, drinking rum and orange juice (his idea of a breakfast of champions). He was a bloody mess.

"What the *fuck* do you guys want?" he croaked.

I grinned. "We had some fun last night, didn't we, Dennis?"

Stan growled, "This is just a reminder, cuz, that we'll be back at any time, day or night, if we ever hear that you bother Brian again. And make no mistake, Rocky and I will be the first ones Brian's nurse will call if you ever show your face at Brian's place again."

I started off joking. "Other than that, Dennis, we love ya! Ya know, you ought to go surfing today. The salt water is great for cuts. Surf's up, Dennis! Don't be a hodad."

My tone shifted as I got serious, "Oh, that's right, I almost forgot. You're a drug addict, not a surfer anymore. So, get this—and get it *good*—LEAVE BRIAN ALONE!"

Dennis didn't want to press charges, because he didn't want the local Venice police to learn of his heavy drug use and the shady goings-on at his house. We had beaten Dennis so severely, though, his lawyer finally convinced him to file a complaint against us in nearby Santa Monica city court. When the charges against us were read in court—breaking and entering, assault and battery—we were asked to enter our pleas.

I stood up. "Guilty as charged, your Honor, with an explanation, if I may."

California Feelin'

The judge said, "Proceed."

"Stan Love and I worked for Dennis's brother, Brian Wilson of the Beach Boys. We had the responsibility of keeping drugs out of Brian's life. We did that for three years, and although we no longer work for Brian in that capacity, we heard that he was in trouble. We learned that Dennis had been giving Brian cocaine on a regular basis. The situation got so bad that Brian suffered a seizure and his caregiver had to manually keep him from swallowing his tongue and possibly choking to death. We no longer work for Brian, but we still love him."

Turning to Dennis, I looked at him and said quietly, "Dennis, you should try that sometime, *loving* Brian." Turning back to face the judge, I continued, "We beat Dennis up, and we'll do it again if Dennis persists on trying to kill Brian, a man who has permanent brain damage from taking too many drugs. Do what you want to Stan and me, but our promise to Dennis remains the same: *Leave Brian alone, or we will be back!*"

A groundswell of murmuring support filled the courtroom. The judge silenced it with his gavel and cleared his throat. "Perhaps there should be more people like you and Mr. Love in this world. I'm going to have to fine the two of you the minimum for breaking and entering, $250 each, plus $500 additional from Mr. Love for the beating that he gave Mr. Wilson.

The judge fixed his gaze on Dennis, "Mr. Wilson, though you are the plaintiff in this case, I truly hope I do not see you in my courtroom again."

Dennis croaked plaintively, "I got beat up for nothing."

I walked over to Dennis, got in his face and said, "You keep doing drugs, Dennis, and you'll be hearing voices just like Brian."

My on-again, off-again roommate and best friend, Stan Love, with his cousin Brian Wilson. Stan was Brian's workout companion, close friend, bodyguard, and life coach.
Photo by Stan Love
from the Larry Salisbury Collection

After our court date, Stan and I admitted to Stephen just how brutal we'd been with Dennis. We wanted his take on the whole dark and scary side of the Brian-Dennis relationship, which damn sure wasn't a pretty one. Stephen had spent many years in close proximity to the brothers, and he'd intervened dozens of times.

Stephen helped us to understand the dynamics and have a little more empathy. Yes, Dennis had always preyed on his vulnerable older brother, but he was in the grip of alcohol and drug addiction and wasn't really in control of his actions.

Stephen believed if Dennis could have done better, he would have, and when Stan and I paid our little visit to Dennis' beach house, we were, as they say in addiction circles, "talking to the disease, not the man."

I was relieved when Stephen went on to say that excusable or not, Dennis' behavior was killing Brian, and only extreme measures on our part had a chance of getting through Dennis' ferocious addiction.

Happily, it looked as though our almost-lethal beating did get through to Dennis. Though we ended up in court (as we well deserved), we had no regrets. Dennis never bothered Brian again.

Chapter Twenty-Two

Wheaties—What The Big Boys Eat

The inspiration I gained working with The Beach Boys helped me launch an extraordinary career and lifestyle.

In 1983, I was cast as a football player for a Wheaties commercial titled "What the Big Boys Eat." My face went onto the front of the Wheaties box, for which I was paid an additional $5,000, and I received $2,000 more for a poster that Wheaties sold from the back of the box. As far as I know, I'm one of the few non-famous pro athletes to ever get onto the front of the Wheaties box.

The Wheaties commercial was shot using a semi-pro football team as extras. I was slated to be the running back, and I flew out to New York with another male model from L.A. who was cast as the quarterback.

When we took the field and started throwing the football around, it was obvious to the director and producers that the ersatz quarterback couldn't throw a football. It was embarrassing, especially to the people who had cast the guy. The guys on the semi-pro team were falling down, they were laughing so hard.

The Beach Boys' Endless Wave

Because I could throw the ball, the director switched me to quarterback, but we discovered the other model couldn't catch the ball either. Before he could be replaced by one of the extras, the poor guy ran into a defender and went down with a knee injury. He had to be carried off the field on a stretcher. After that, all he was good for was close-ups. The next day they shot him eating Wheaties out of a bowl, dribbling milk down his chin, with his leg in a cast.

When the shoot wrapped, I called a photographer named Herb Zane whom I had met years before in Hawaii. He had taken some beach shots of me, and he told me to look him up if I was ever in New York. Herb took me to dinner that night in the West Village, and said I could crash at his place on 54th Street near Eighth Avenue. When I asked if Studio 54 was on the same street, Herb said indeed it was, and he'd be glad to take me there after dinner.

Studio 54 had seen better days, but Herb said it could still be a bit dicey getting in

As far as I know, I'm one of the few non-famous pro athletes ever to get onto the front of the Wheaties box...

Photo courtesy of General Mills

WHEATIES—WHAT THE BIG BOYS EAT

unless you were "on the list" or knew one of the doormen. Happily, the woman guarding the door gave me a big smile, lifted the red rope, and let us in. Herb laughed, "Are things *always* this easy for you?"

That evening, I met Carol, a beautiful model from Lexington, Kentucky. I took her to dinner the following night, and she suggested that while I'm in New York I stay at her upper Westside apartment. It was near Café des Artistes in a quieter neighborhood than Herb's; Carol was very convincing.

...and I made a splash on the back of the box too.
Photo courtesy of General Mills

The next day I told Herb I decided to stay in New York a while longer—at Carol's uptown apartment. He shook his head, "I guess things *do* come easy for you."

CHAPTER TWENTY-THREE

We Lose Dennis

I had been in New York for a few months when Stephen and Stan called me from the Kona ranch on a speaker phone. Without preamble, they told me Dennis had died.

"Holy shit! What? Are you kidding me?"

"He drowned yesterday." Stan said, flatly. "In fifteen feet of water in Marina del Rey, around 5:30 p.m., just three weeks after his 39th birthday."

I was stunned, especially that Dennis had *drowned*. He was an accomplished swimmer and surfer, fearless in the water. After my initial shock, the three of us talked with much sadness about Dennis and the tragedy.

We later learned his blood alcohol level was 0.26, nearly three times the legal limit allowed for driving a car—and this was in the afternoon, mind you, after eating a turkey sandwich and taking a nap, according to his friends. Dennis was partying on a boat parked next to the empty slip where his beloved sailboat, *Harmony*, had been moored until the IRS seized it for unpaid taxes.

Though it was December and the Pacific was frigid (only in the 50s), Dennis repeatedly dived into the cold water and swam down to the bottom, looking for stuff he had thrown overboard during the many fights he had with his volatile ex-wife. Dennis told anyone who would listen that there was buried treasure in the murky depths below: expensive jewelry, art, and valuable personal memorabilia.

Like all marinas in protected harbors, the wooden walkways between slips are only a foot or two above water level, depending on the tide. Dennis was wearing a diving mask to help him see what he was attempting to retrieve from the dark sea floor. He held his breath while diving below the surface, then came up for more air as needed. Perhaps he got cramps from ignoring the old adage about not swimming for an hour after eating. He *did* have that turkey sandwich after taking his nap, and Dennis Wilson wasn't prone to waiting when he set his mind on doing something. Patience was not one of his virtues.

Most probably, he hit his head on the underside of a wooden walkway while coming up for air, knocking himself out. Stephen guessed that Dennis got disoriented, as most drunks do in the water, and hit his head, if not on the walkway, then possibly on the underside of one of the boats moored in the slips adjacent to his former boat's berth.

No matter how it happened, Dennis Wilson, the only Beach Boy who ever actually surfed, a lifelong ocean lover, drowned in fifteen feet of water. This was the same Beach Boy who had befriended Charlie Manson and let the Manson Family live for a year at his palatial log cabin at 14400 Sunset Blvd.

When Dennis was flush in the late Sixties and living a life of wild abandon, he rented the log cabin that once belonged to humorist Will Rogers. Drugs and orgies were the order of the day; it was a period in Dennis' life that he later admitted helped destroy him, even financially. He claimed that the Manson family took him for at least $100,000. Eventually, Dennis and

WE LOSE DENNIS

Dennis Wilson, reflective and all alone by the Pacific Ocean he loved so much. Brian Wilson survived his battle with drug addiction. Dennis Wilson, sadly, in the end, did not.

Photo by and courtesy of Dean Torrence

Charlie had a falling out, and Charlie and his harem left some time before the Tate-LaBianca murders in August, 1969.

The murders freaked out all of Hollywood. Frightened and paranoid, Dennis thought Charlie was looking for him, and he hid out until Charlie was finally arrested. Dennis' association with Manson always haunted him.

And now Dennis had drowned in his beloved Pacific Ocean Blue; that was the name of his solo album. It was produced by James Guercio, the manager and producer for Chicago, the successful jazz-rock band. Guercio and CBS Records had given

Dennis a $100,000 budget to make the record. Dennis wrote and sang all the songs on the album, and it got good reviews, though it only spent 12 weeks on the charts.

Long after Dennis died, *MOJO*, the English equivalent of *Rolling Stone*, claimed *Pacific Ocean Blue* was a bona fide masterpiece. I just wish Dennis could have lived long enough to learn that his solo album is revered by the British music world. It would have meant the world to him.

The irony of the blue Pacific Ocean claiming this surfer's life was foremost on the minds of Stephen, Stan, and me, and probably many others.

"You know, Rocky, you were right," Stephen said. "You were the one who said Dennis would never live to see 40, that he was a modern-day James Dean type, and here he is dead at 39."

As we reminisced, Stephen talked about how seriously Dennis had deteriorated the last few years of his life. The Beach Boys had tried to employ tough love to save Dennis. They threw him into rehab half a dozen times, and it never worked. Each time he would stay for a few days, get some strength back, and then just walk out. He was reduced to begging his brothers to let him tour with the band again and make some money, which he desperately needed.

The last time he asked to rejoin the band, he was told he had to stay the entire 28 days in the rehab facility that they were paying for, or they would kick him out of the Beach Boys for good. Being in the Beach Boys was everything to Dennis, his raison d'être. He *loved* being a Beach Boy.

But even with their threat to fire him, he lasted less than a week at the last rehab place. He escaped in the middle of the night and went to the flophouse hotel where his teenage wife

We Lose Dennis

was staying with their son, across the street from his favorite Venice Beach watering hole, Chez Jay's.

Dennis had a volatile relationship with his young wife (his fourth). When he forced his way into her motel room in the middle of the night, two of her friends beat him up and kicked him down the stairs. Having nowhere to go, Dennis limped across the street to Chez Jay's.

In his last months, Dennis' alcohol and drug consumption had escalated beyond being just out of control, and his rational decision-making was at its lowest ebb. He was spiraling out of control; he was headed toward a suicidal crash and burn. Dennis, reeling in a stupor from one moment to the next, was the only one who didn't realize it.

I asked Stephen, "Did Stan ever tell you about the time we took Brian to somebody's place in Malibu to celebrate his mother's birthday?"

He hadn't heard, so I continued. "All the Beach Boys were there and about twenty other people. It was a nice family barbecue. Everybody was seated in the family room and we had started eating. Just as I sat down in a recliner with a plateful of ribs, beans, and potato salad on my lap, Dennis appeared out of nowhere with a pool cue, and he slammed it down hard on my plate of food, then ran out the back door.

"Nobody moved. I was *outraged*. I jumped up and chased after Dennis, but Stan blocked me at the back door and begged me not to beat up Dennis in front of his mom on her birthday. I was so incensed, I shrugged him off and charged out the back door.

"Dennis was trapped in the yard, and when he realized he had nowhere to run, he rushed up to me, hugged me, and said, 'I love you, man.'

"I shook my head and said in a voice loud enough for everyone to hear, 'Dennis, that is so chickenshit, man. What a bunch of shit! You slam a pool cue down on my plate of food and then tell me you love me so I won't kick your ass. Is that the way you go through life?'"

Stephen was furious. "Chickenshit is right. Dennis knew the people there wouldn't let you beat him up in front of his mother—especially on her birthday."

Stan added, "You *had* to let him slide that time, man."

"Yeah, I had to let the little shit slide that time, but he got his in the end. I saw a much different-looking Dennis just before I came to New York, just a few months ago."

I told them the whole sordid story. I had just left a friend's place and was driving those little back streets by the Santa Monica pier, when I saw a short guy with a shaved head. God, I couldn't believe it was Dennis; he looked like a derelict. When I called out to him, he screamed, 'Fuck you, Rocky!' and flipped me off with both hands.

I followed him and said, "Come on, Dennis. Get in. I'll give you a ride." I was completely amazed when he did. He got in and said, "Let's go to Chez Jay's, asshole."

He smelled terrible and looked even worse. He had cuts and scrapes on his face, hands, arms and feet. I said, "Okay. Chez Jay's it is, they have great mai tais, and it's just up the street and around the corner."

When we walked in, the bartender shouted, "Damn, Dennis, did you get the license plate number of the truck that hit you? You look like shit. And you didn't pay your tab again last night."

Dennis said, "I'll get you your money, asshole, as soon as I get back from touring. Now give us two mai tais!"

We Lose Dennis

"Who are you calling an asshole? I ought to throw your sorry ass . . ." Before he could say, "out," I pulled out a twenty and put it on the bar, and he snatched it up and made us the mai tais.

Dennis demanded, "Put a float of Myers' dark rum on those." The bartender had already done so, but he added a little extra. Dennis practically chugged his down and ordered two more. Talk about entitlement issues! Talk about really needing a drink.

I asked Dennis, "So what's with the shaved head, man?"

"Punk rock. Don't you know nuthin'?"

"I know someone just beat the shit out of you recently."

Dennis didn't say anything until he chugged his second mai tai, ordered more, and chugged that one down too, then he jumped up off the stool he was sitting on, pointed outside the door, and croaked, "Yeah, my fuckin' wife had me beat up. I'm gonna go back over there and show her fuckin' ass."

The bartender spoke up then. "Okay, that's *it*, Dennis. You can't talk like that in here. You're out of here, Dennis. You're eighty-sixed. And don't come back until you can pay your $200 bar tab, and I'm dead serious this time."

Dennis screamed, "Fuck you! I made this place. I made Chez Jay's famous. I'm the Beach Boys. This place would be nothing without me and you know it. Fuck you and your shitty little dive bar! I've been thrown out of better places than this!"

I practically carried Dennis out of the place. Before I could blink an eye, he charged right out into the street. I didn't have a chance to grab him. He jaywalked his way straight across Ocean Avenue, which was crammed with rush hour traffic. He was nearly hit by a few cars, which screeched to a halt. Cars were honking at the baldheaded, barefoot vagrant who was defying cars to hit him as he marched across the crowded four-lane street in rush hour traffic without looking either way while staring straight ahead, totally oblivious. He was a man on a mission.

I ended the sad story with some regret. "I knew Dennis was going to get beat up again, if he even made it across the street alive. I wanted to help him, to stop him. I really did, but there was no way I was risking my own safety going out in that traffic. So, I just stood there and watched Mr. Hollywood nearly get himself run over. He was a one-man wrecking crew hellbent on self-destruction. He was on a dead-end mission. He had no fear. He had nothing. I wish I'd known that was the last time I would ever see Dennis alive."

There was silence on the phone, then Stephen said, "You know, Rocky, Dennis did have some good points. You only knew him these last few years. He was a terrific show drummer. While Brian called him a clubber and used Hal Blaine from the Wrecking Crew on the recordings, Dennis worked very hard on the road. He kept the driving, pulsating beat going for the Beach Boys for many, many years . . . and he always looked good doing it. Dennis was perhaps the most handsome drummer in all of rock and roll. The girls would always scream for him, and they threw themselves at him in droves. Dennis never lacked for female company.

"I saw up close just how hard the man worked, how he would come off the stage after a show completely drenched in sweat. He was physically beautiful, and his nightly workouts on those drums kept him fit and strong. He was the embodiment of the lean, chiseled surfer dude. To top it off, Dennis' thick hair was perfect.

"I prefer to remember Dennis as the charismatic rock and roll icon that he once was before the drugs and alcohol led to his demise."

"Amen to that," I said.

Looking back, decades later, I think one of Dennis' best epitaphs wasn't words, it was the mural at Danny's in Venice Beach, a place that recently closed, unfortunately. The painting showed Dennis drinking coffee in his beloved neighborhood, perched next to Jim Morrison, Janis Joplin, and other famed local musicians who lived too hard and died too young.

I admit, though, that every time I saw the mural, I couldn't resist wondering what type of booze he'd poured into that cup. You can be sure that Dennis Wilson would never have just plain, black coffee in *his* cup.

Chapter Twenty-Four

Mike and the Prince

Tony Graham was another New York friend, one of my L.A. roommates when I first started modeling. A former UCLA tennis player, Tony was a member at the right gym, the Vertical Club, which I joined for a mere thousand 1983-era dollars. Whew! I quickly learned that things aren't cheap in New York.

A couple of months later, Tony invited Carol and me to have dinner with a small group of folks he knew, including Prince Albert of Monaco and his three female companions. Tony had become friends with the prince when they won a doubles match in a Monte Carlo tennis tournament the year before.

I called Stan and told him I'd been invited to have dinner with Prince Albert the following weekend. Stan called back the next day, and asked, "Do you think you can get Mike invited, too? He plans to be in New York over the weekend."

I knew Mike would enjoy this type of event and could be trusted to act like a gentleman, not like some other rock stars I'd met. I ran the idea by Tony, and he thought Mike Love would be a good fit, since Prince Albert liked to hobnob with celebrities. Mike was invited, along with his date.

It was arranged that we would all meet at the famous Oak Room bar in the Plaza Hotel for cocktails at 7:30, and then move on to the very formal, expensive Le Cirque for dinner at 9.

By this time, I had moved out of Carol's place and had my own pad on East 57th Street and Lexington Avenue. I invited Mike and his date Lulu to swing by my place to meet Carol and have a cocktail, and then the four of us walked three blocks to the Oak Room.

We arrived on time, and, as was to be expected, the Prince and his entourage arrived ten minutes late. We were seated at a large private booth by the window facing the park, with a good view of the carriages trotting by on Central Park South.

Prince Albert spoke to Tony in almost a whisper, asking him how his tennis game was going. Tony answered modestly, "My game is still a work in progress. Our doubles victory in Monte Carlo is the highlight of my not-so-successful career."

The Prince casually acknowledged their victory and said, "Oh yes, winning is always fun."

I recognized one of the prince's three companions from a party I had attended the weekend before, so I smiled, "Hi, I remember meeting you at Vincent's last Friday."

The pretty lady didn't say anything at first. She looked at Albert, who reluctantly nodded his permission, and she said, "Yes, I remember meeting you."

I decided introductions were in order, and said, "Say hello to Carol—and this is Mike and Lulu." Everyone nodded without saying anything. I thought this was kind of strange, and added, "Don't everyone talk at once. *Ouch!*"

I turned to Tony, "First you step on my toe and now you pinch me. What the hell, man!" Dead silence followed that remark. You could hear a pin drop.

Mike and the Prince

The prince finally whispered something to one of his escorts, who whispered something to one of the other girls, who whispered to the girl I had addressed, all of whom seemed to be sitting on their hands.

Mike was noticeably silent, too, which wasn't like him. I muttered to him, "What are *you* so quiet about?" He looked at me, smiled, and didn't say a word. Guess he'd looked up appropriate behavior around so-called royalty. *I* sure didn't give a damn.

A bottle of Cristal champagne was served. I toasted Carol, then whispered in her ear, "This is the worst non-conversation I've ever had. I wonder if we can get out of dinner."

When we arrived at the glaringly formal French restaurant, we did manage to have a dinner conversation with the prince, thank God, though it was as boring and stilted as I've ever heard. If Mike and Lulu hadn't been there to talk to, I wouldn't have made it through the main course. As far as I was concerned, Mike was the prince at that table.

After dessert, the prince asked Mike, "Are the Beach Boys still touring?"

Mike answered modestly, "We still do selective dates."

I laughed. "You're just being modest, Mike." I turned to the prince. "When I was with Brian, the Beach Boys did over a hundred gigs in a year. At one of them, Carl was so drunk he fell backwards into the drums and sent Dennis sprawling. Dennis wandered offstage swearing to himself, waving his hands and arms in the air like Don Quixote."

The prince let out a little girlish titter. I concluded my story, "These guys, especially Mike, can still rock it with the best of them."

I paused a beat, stood up, and announced, "Hey, listen,

Carol and I gotta go. We're meeting some friends. See you around, Albert. Don't get up. Later, Tony, Robert. See ya, Mike. Nice to meet you, Lulu." I whirled Carol out of there. The prince's tableful of guests didn't say a word, not even "farewell."

The following night, Carol and I were supposed to meet at one of those super-trendy snobby doorman clubs near Union Square. As I got out of a cab, I saw Prince Albert, of all people, walking down the steps from the front door. He was fuming at the doorman, and I heard him growl, "You have *no* idea what a big mistake you have just made."

At that moment, his eyes met mine. He didn't say a word; he stopped dead in his tracks for a couple of seconds, then he stormed down the stairs and deliberately bumped into me. The prince didn't even bother to say, "Excuse me!" I should have grabbed him by the back of his bleached blond hair, and said, "Say 'excuse me' or I'm gonna pull your hair out." I had no idea he'd soon go bald *without* my help.

Instead, I laughed and headed up the stairs to Norman the doorman, who greeted me warmly as he opened the door. I looked back at the prince; he looked even more outraged, if that was possible. I paused and asked Norman, "Do you know who that is?"

"He said that he's some prince, but he's not on the list."

"He is indeed a prince. That, my friend, is Prince Albert of Monaco. I had dinner with him and some friends last night. He was rude as hell then, too."

The doorman said nervously, "Oh shit. Is he really a prince? I screwed up. Do you want to bring him in with you?"

I looked at Prince Albert, who was still steaming mad, standing next to his limo. "Nah. He's an asshole. Besides, he has a pain in the ass protocol you're supposed to follow—

you're not supposed to talk unless he talks to you first. Plus, he's a big drag."

The doorman laughed, "He's Prince Albert, he's no fun, and he's a big drag?"

Everybody waiting in line got a big laugh out of that. Someone called out, "He looks more like a drag queen."

Prince Albert roared, "You will *never* work in this town again!"

I asked Norman, "Is he talking to you or me?

As I walked through the door that had been closed to the prince, I thought about the night that Dennis Wilson was turned away by two doorman, and how he fearlessly and stupidly charged them and got his throat ruined. Maybe there was something to royal manners after all. Albert may have lost his dignity, but at least he walked away unscathed.

The next night when I stopped back by the same club and found a different doorman, I learned just how brutal so-called royal manners could be. Dennis was rough, but he'd never stab the doormen in the back.

"Where's Norman?" I asked the new guy.

"Oh, um, he got fired."

"*What?* Why?"

"For not letting some prince in last night.".

I was taken aback by this news. "You're kidding!"

"No, it was in the paper and everything today."

"I was here last night. I saw the whole thing. The prince wasn't even on the list. Norman was just doing his job."

"Yeah, the girl that makes up the list didn't put the prince on it. She thought it was some kinda bogus reservation."

"Well, why didn't they fire the girl instead?"

"Uh, the girl is screwing the boss."

"So, let me get this straight," I mused aloud. "The girl who screwed up the reservation is screwing the boss, so the boss didn't fire the girl he's screwing—instead he fired poor Norman, who basically got screwed for doing his job."

"Yep, that pretty much sums it up. Norman got screwed."

"Norman got screwed and he didn't even get kissed." I concluded sadly.

Chapter Twenty-Five

Europe

In late 1983, right around the time I moved to New York and Dennis died, Stan called me to say he and his girlfriend were getting tired of island life and planned to move back to the mainland soon.

He moved into the house we owned together and took over the mortgage payments, which took a load off my back. After about nine months, he told me he'd found a buyer for the house, if I would agree to sell. I thought about it, and decided it was a good idea to not be tied down.

My life became more fluid, moving back and forth between New York and Los Angeles, depending on the modeling and acting gig I landed. For the next couple of years, I worked my ass off and made the most of the gifts I was given.

I had always wanted to bum around Europe, and in 1986, when I had some money in the bank and a few free months, I decided to make the trip before another excuse got in my way. My first stop was Rome, where I knew a publicist named Chuck. He had worked on *Ben Hur* more than 25 years before, and he never left Rome after the movie wrapped. A few years earlier, Chuck had extended an open invitation to visit, and now I decided to accept his offer of hospitality.

Chuck gave me an overview of Rome, showing me around the city on a friend's scooter, or motorino. He told me I should get one of my own and really explore the fabled city, if I was going to stay awhile.

I bought myself a motorino, and Chuck introduced me to his friend, Anabella, who generously let me rent one of her rooms. Anabella was a splendid cook, though modest about her culinary skills. She showed me the best scenic views of the city and introduced me to the neighborhood. We lived next to an old abbey that had become a park, and it had an unobstructed view of the Vatican as well as the other six famous hilltop landmarks with their cathedrals, monuments, towers, and large statues of Jesus.

A couple of blocks away, Chuck's palazzo was within sight of the magnificent Trevi Fountain and close to the famous Spanish Steps. Rome was the perfect place to start my European adventures.

I had been in Rome for six weeks when I ran into Mike Romano, a model-actor friend I knew from L.A., and his girlfriend, Sabella. Mike insisted that we investigate Rome properly. For an entire week, we zipped around on our scooters, visiting the most famous and historic sites, including some unique, out-of-the-way and not-so-obvious places. Since Mike read the travel literature on everything we visited, I had a fascinating time, and his running commentary was priceless.

We made sure we investigated Rome's night life, too. Mike's best friend, Bootsy, owned the nicest nightclub in Rome, and the three of us became regulars. Bootsy treated us like royalty—and we never got a check for more than $20.

After a few weeks, Mike and Sabella took off to visit his mother in St. Tropez, and they insisted that I come along. I

Europe

decided I'd spent enough time in Rome, so I said goodbye to Chuck and Anabella, sold my scooter, and left for France with Mike and his girlfriend.

We took the ferry, eating gambon and fromage paninis (ham and cheese sandwiches) and sipping white wine en route. I hadn't seen the Mediterranean since my all-too-brief vacation with Brian, Marilyn, and Stan in 1977, and I was happy to be back.

Mike's mother, Monique, was a true gem—a real treasure, a great beauty, and a fantastic dancer. Her marvelous hillside villa overlooked the surreal French coastline. It was as beautiful as I remembered.

The night sky lit the Mediterranean shoreline with a million twinkling stars; it felt as though you could see forever. The scent of nearby pine trees and flowers perfumed the air. Monique's villa had, without a doubt, one of the greatest views I had ever seen, and it was in one of the most desirable locations on the French Riviera.

The next morning, Mike and Sabella dropped me off at Club 55, a posh beach club and the local hangout spot for Americans. You knew you reached Club 55 when you saw a little white wooden sign at the end of a long narrow winding road with "55" printed on it in large red numbers, and "You are here" written with a black magic marker at the bottom.

It was early morning and I was the first person there, so I took a long walk down the enchanting French beach that I had admired the night before in the moonlight.

I returned a couple of hours later, asked the poolside bartender for a cold beer, and heard, "Hey, Rocky!"

It was John Rockwell, a longtime party friend from L.A. John, a former lifeguard at the Beverly Hills Hotel, had made his way up in L.A. society by being very outgoing and helpful. He also had a unique talent for remembering the name of everyone he met.

John was a regular guest at Hugh Hefner's Playboy mansion, a rarity for a non-celebrity, especially a male. He was also on the A-list at the Forum Club, owned by the Lakers' owner, Jerry Buss, and frequented by Jack Nicholson and many other Hollywood celebrities. John was a high-rolling gambler and a backgammon whiz, and he was in the middle of a game. He courteously introduced me to his opponent, but the charmless fellow must have been losing. He didn't say hi or shake hands; he just growled, "Are we gonna play or are we gonna socialize?"

John's current girlfriend, Suzy, had just done a centerfold layout for Playboy magazine and, being a generous girl, she was happy to finance their trip. Suzy was content to hang by the pool tanning herself while John played backgammon with the richest man in the world, according to the then-current issue of Forbes magazine. The billionaire was also a fat guy who needed a lesson in manners.

I hung out by the pool with Suzy; who doesn't want to hang out with a Playboy bunny who's wearing a bikini? (Of course, I was only there because she was such a good conversationalist.) It wasn't long before my history with the Beach Boys came up and I found myself chatting about them with her and the rather social crowd around us.

A guitar aficionado was in the group, a huge Carl Wilson fan. He was right on when he raved about Carl's transporting guitar solos, which are legendary. I was happy to tell him about something really valuable Carl did for the Beach Boys that most people don't know.

Europe

When Brian Wilson abruptly stopped touring with the band in late 1964, it was Carl who stepped up and filled the musical leadership void Brian left behind. Mike Love was the overall leader and he really ran the show, but, in purely the musical sense, Carl had the mojo to fill Brian's shoes. He was more than able.

Carl undertook his new role without hesitation. Yeah, he did like to drink a bit, and he and Dennis could be rowdy and undependable from time to time, but he could sing like an angel and play like a rock star.

At the end of the day, John had a big smile on his face. We were all invited up to the rich guy's villa—not for more backgammon, the games would resume tomorrow—but for a lobster feast with all the trimmings, and, of course, much fine French wine. What more does anyone need, I asked myself, but more of the same? And that's exactly what we got for the next glorious week—more, more, and *more*.

When Mike and Sabella picked me up at Club 55 one afternoon, I introduced them to John and Suzy. They hit it off, and we had a cold beer together. We got together a couple of hours later for a stroll along the yacht harbor to see what trouble we could get into. We also planned to have more drinks, followed by dinner on the wharf.

We were ambling down the wharf past rows of magnificent yachts, and I heard, "Rocky!" Grace Robbins, my long-time friend from L.A., was waving from her giant yacht, *Gracia*. She was married to Harold Robbins, author of almost thirty novels including *The Carpetbagger* and *Nevada Smith*. I'd read all Harold's books; Grace had given me a complete set some time ago.

The five of us were welcomed aboard, and Grace hugged

me warmly as I made introductions; I wasn't surprised that she already knew John Rockwell. Champagne was served, and everyone reminisced about places we had all seen and people we had met. As a part-time St. Tropez resident, Mike charmed Grace with his local knowledge, and John was trying to get a backgammon game going.

Sabella linked arms with me and walked me to the aft deck. She asked with a saucy grin, "Are you a gigolo?"

I laughed. "I *don't* think so."

"I don't think so, either. If you were, you'd be living on this yacht."

"Well, the night is still young." We hugged and shared a good laugh. She also shared a nicely rolled joint of locally grown pot with me. The vibe was serene and mellow.

Grace invited us to continue the evening at a party at the Byblos Hotel. In the limo on our way to the hotel, I told them about my visit to the Byblos nine years earlier, and Brian Wilson's drug-induced meltdown at the hotel's poolside bar. I choked up. "It was like he had a nervous breakdown right in front of all these strangers. He was a babbling wreck."

Grace reached out, put her arm around me, and said, "I think I know how you feel. Several people close to me have had similar experiences."

John added, "Same here, Rocky. The trick, I've learned, is not to let the party get the best of you. You have to know when to leave. You never want to be the last one at the fair."

Mike and Sabella were looking at me. Sabella asked, "Who is Brian Wilson?"

"He's one of the Beach Boys."

Sabella shrieked, "Oh, I love the Beach Boys! What happened to him at the poolside bar? Is Brian all right?"

"Is Brian all right? Well, that's a matter of interpretation. As to what happened? I guess, maybe too much of everything," I mused aloud.

"*Too much* is what has gotten the best of too many people," Grace murmured.

"So, is Brian okay now?" Sabella asked again.

"Who knows? I haven't seen him in years. He did call me up six months after I stopped working for him, and he insisted that I come over to his pad for a barbecue. We played the piano and sang songs all afternoon. Then the next weekend he showed up at my house in his Cadillac convertible, and took me for a cruise up the coast to Malibu. We laughed and talked like brothers for hours. That was the last time I saw him."

Wistfully, I added, "I should have called him back, or just stopped by from time to time, but he was into partying. When I worked for him, my job was to keep booze and drugs *out* of his life, not to share them with him. Something about partying with him just didn't feel right to me."

John was surprised. "I didn't think Brian even drove a car anymore."

"He didn't when I worked for him, and hadn't for years before that. I was shocked to see him behind the wheel by himself, especially at my house."

Grace remarked, "He must have cared for you, Rocky."

John added, "He called you and had you over for a barbecue? And then the next weekend he drove to your house by himself and wanted you to go for a cruise with him? He definitely likes you, Rocky, unless he was taking you out to have you bumped off. Just joking, bro. Let's party!"

"Yeah, let's go party!" Grace enthused.

Mike and Sabella chimed in, "Let's party!"

I wrapped it up, "That's what *I* always say. The party must go on."

After a few more days, the billionaire lost big to John and split. Word of John's skill had spread, and he couldn't pick up a backgammon game with anyone. Looking for new opportunities, John, Suzy, and I rented a car and drove over to Cannes for a few days. In the evenings, John put on an Armani tuxedo and played at the Carlton Hotel bar lounge. It was dark and luxurious in there, and it was game on! Backgammon tables were jam-packed throughout the enormous lounge. John had to wait an hour to get a game most nights.

During the day, it was the same routine at the beach in front of the Carlton. We'd rent an umbrella, beach chairs, and towels, and it was game on all day long, too. After three days of this action, John was still sporting a smile, but he said to me, "The important thing about backgammon is knowing how much to bet, when to bet, and when not to bet. But, the *most* important thing is to know when to quit and when to leave."

"Uh-oh. Is this 'so long,' John?"

"Yep. It's that time, my friend," John pulled out a watch he had loaned me earlier. "Here, I want you to have this."

"John, I can't take that."

John would not be deterred. "You can, and you will. You brought me luck, man. Look, I'm pretty good at backgammon. I am. But I'd rather be lucky than good any day. I was down big time, and my luck changed for the better when you walked into Club 55. And I've been lucky ever since—real lucky. Those rich guys like to go double or nothing when they're losing. It's called 'buying the table.' And it takes big cojones not to fold. And now, my good-luck friend, it's time for me to leave."

"Quit while you're ahead and save your cojones?"

"You got it—always better to go home a winner." John laughed and slapped me on the back.

John and Suzy caught the next flight back to Los Angeles. When we parted, I told John that I would call him when I got back home. To be truthful, I didn't know *where* home was anymore. I decided to stop in London for a few days.

The last time I left St. Tropez, I was with Stan and the Wilsons, and we took limousines and flew first class. This time I went the budget route, and I decided to take a train to Paris and connect to the pre-Chunnel train ferry.

Going through Paris triggered some good memories of my time there with Brian and Marilyn, but this trip there'd be no dinner at the Ritz. Instead, I partied on the train with some American college kids.

Once in London, I checked into a pension near Hyde Park which was filled with many of the same American college kids who'd been on the train with me. That night, I went to the Hippodrome club, and I stood in line with a couple dozen other people waiting to get in. When it was my turn to enter, the cashier told me that the guy in front of me had paid my cover. I caught up with the couple, introduced myself to Sid and Nancy, and insisted on buying them a drink. Sid refused, saying that he and his wife were on vacation from Miami, they were rich, and they insisted on buying.

I grinned. "Do I have 'I'm poor' written on my forehead?"

They laughed, "No." Nancy went on to say they were staying on a yacht on the Thames, in central London, and invited me to a party they were throwing the next night.

Before the night was over, I had piqued the interest of Felicia, the singer-guitarist who was performing at the club. My newfound friends and I were having so much fun that we all decided to have a nightcap on the yacht. Sid and Nancy insisted that Felicia and I spend the night onboard, and they told me to invite the college students to their yacht party the next night.

The following day, Felicia and I took the students to lunch at McDonald's. They were jumping up and down with excitement when we agreed to meet at the pension at 5:00 p.m. and go to the yacht party from there.

On the yacht that night, one of the girls in the group found out I'd been intimately associated with the Beach Boys. Word spread and things got a little nutty. One girls squealed, "Omigod! Dennis and Mike! So hot! When I was in high school, I didn't know which one was sexier!"

I chuckled to myself. The long-standing competition between Mike and Dennis for Beach Boys sex symbol was legendary, and this would have driven them both nuts.

We started talking music, which always makes me happy. The kids asked if I'd toured with the Beach Boys, and I shared some stories. They enjoyed hearing about Dennis' antics, which were less annoying in the retelling. I also told them about Brian's huge, emotional "Brian's Back" welcome at the record label event just a few miles from where we were floating on the Thames.

The students asked me to go to Liverpool and visit old Beatles' haunts with them the next evening, and I was sorely tempted. It was hard to pass up, but money was getting tight. My instincts told me it was time to leave. Maybe I had learned something from John Rockwell.

After I saw my new friends off the following evening, I went to Piccadilly Square, where I found a pub and ordered a warm beer. Ugh. While I choked down the beer, I struck up a conversation with an interesting-looking guy from Perth, Australia, and found he'd actually been at one of the Beach

Europe

Boys concerts in 1978 when we were "down under."

He was a pretty observant guy, and he wondered who was on stage doing the drumming that night. He knew it wasn't Dennis Wilson. He was right. It was one of those nights when Dennis had gone off on a tear and backup drummer Mike Kowalski had to fill in, often at a second's notice, right in the middle of a set.

Kowalski was a really interesting guy and a heck of a good drummer, but he didn't have a position I would have wanted. It was no easy task being the guy who had to step in for Dennis; that surely meant that Dennis was good and drunk or massively stoned, mean as hell, and in no mood to be trifled with.

No one ever knew when Dennis would flare up, Dennis-style. At the very least, he'd never willingly give up his post without a scene. Kowalski had a quiet, laid-back personality that made him perfect for the job. He also looked a lot like Dennis from the other side of the lights.

I happily accepted when he invited me to a garden party on the roof of a nearby hotel and sipped a glass of white wine as I strolled around the garden's fountains and koi-filled interlinking ponds.

I heard, "Rocky!" It was Paul Jabara, the actor-songwriter whom I'd met when he played the piano at my friend Doris Carr's New Year's Eve party a few years before. Paul wrote "No More Tears (Enough Is Enough)," a song that Barbra Streisand and Donna Summers recorded as a duet. The song was a monster, a smash hit, and had made him filthy rich.

Paul also wrote "Last Dance," which won him an Oscar and a Grammy award. According to his co-producer and co-writer Bob Esty, Paul locked Donna Summer into a Puerto Rican hotel bathroom and forced her to listen to a tape of him singing

"Last Dance," fortunately for them both.

Paul was with John Schlesinger, the Oscar-winning director of *Midnight Cowboy*. Paul introduced us, and we hung out together the rest of the evening. John invited me to a dinner party he was hosting the following night, a casual affair with a mellow group of eight guests.

The food was simple and delicious, the wines were some of the finest that I had ever tasted, and, to top it all off, there was a little after-dinner pot. The conversation was great, and there was much laughter as well as snifters of brandy and cognac. Did I mention lots of laughter?

John suggested that I stay at his place for a while; Paul and I could pal around together during the day, and at night the three of us could eat, drink, and be merry. This was exactly what we did. The next day I checked out of the pension and moved into John's place on Victoria Street near Piccadilly Square.

The next day, the three of us took a fascinating cruise down the Thames River. We had an enjoyable sack lunch at the turnaround spot, after which we slipped around a corner for a quick couple of tokes.

For weeks, Paul and I gallivanted around London during the daytime, and I helped Noel Davis, John's live-in editor, with the ever-delightful nightly dinner parties. My efforts consisted mainly of picking fresh herbs from the garden.

One night, when Paul was busy, John took me to see *Follies*, the musical, and then we went to The Savoy Hotel for a late supper. John mentioned that the Queen occasionally dined there. We ordered filet of sole with scalloped potatoes and asparagus spears, at John's suggestion, and a nice Pouilly-Fuissé, at my urging.

During dinner, I told John about my two encounters with

Prince Albert in New York. John was barely able to contain his laughter as I related the scenes that took place at the Oak Room and dinner. When I got to the next evening's escapade at the snobby club, John was laughing so hard he had to excuse himself and go to the men's room.

No sooner had John returned, when lo and behold, whom do you think appeared? In walked the Queen of England herself, accompanied by three very sophisticated types, dressed to the nines.

John whispered to me, "Oh, my God, the Queen—she's here! She may come by the table and acknowledge me. After all, I've been knighted."

We stood as Her Royal Highness approached the table and said, "Hello, John. How nice to see you. You're looking well." John kissed the Queen's ring and stammered through the usual pleasantries.

John introduced me as "Rushton, a friend from California." The Queen nodded. I did the same and said nothing. Perhaps I had learned a thing or two since Prince Albert. After all, this was the *Queen*, not some arrogant prince.

As soon as the Queen was led to her table and seated, John excused himself again, saying he had to call Noel Davis and inform him of the Queen's appearance. Noel suddenly appeared as we were finishing our filet of sole, and the three of us had another glass of wine together.

As we left, John again paid his respects to the Queen. He asked, "Your Majesty, do you remember my editor, Noel?"

Queen Elizabeth said graciously, "Of course I do. How are you, Noel?" As we were about to leave, the Queen asked, "Rushton, is this your first visit to London?"

"No, Your Majesty. I have been to London before with the

Beach Boys, in 1977. But I did meet your fellow royal, Prince Albert, in New York in 1984."

"Oh, really. Where might that have been?"

"We had dinner together, then we met again at a private club."

"Oh, that dreadful place that turned poor Albert away."

"Yes. He bumped into me as he was storming down the stairs."

Ever the etiquette-conscious lady, Queen Elizabeth said, "Well, I hope the Prince said, 'excuse me.'" This bon mot elicited light laughter from her entourage.

"Not exactly. He was in a rage and uttering expletives. I'm afraid his tirade didn't include an 'excuse me.'"

More laughter. John spoke up and addressed the Queen. "Well, we must be running along now, Your Majesty." I think John was afraid I might tell Her Majesty about the night at the Oak Room where I violated royal customs, or how I almost grabbed the Prince by the back of his bleached blonde hair.

"John, I'm sending you an invitation to a little art show next weekend. Do bring Noel and your charming friend Rushton."

"We would be delighted.'

After we were out of earshot, John said, "My God, I thought the Queen was going to have a stroke when you brought up Prince Albert's experience at that club. It was in all the papers here—'Prince Snubbed In New York!' It was practically an international scandal."

"Well, it's a good thing I didn't tell the Queen what a bore Albert was the night before."

John grinned, "Well, at least we are not boring."

Chapter Twenty-Six

The Camel Man

Soon after I returned from Europe, I moved back to Los Angeles for good. My friend Sam Albanese picked me up at the airport, and we drove to Chez Jay's on Ocean Avenue in Santa Monica—Dennis Wilson's favorite beach bar, where I'd bought him a couple of drinks about a month before he drowned. When we walked into the joint, I put a twenty on the bar and asked Sam, "How about a mai tai? I'm buying."

Sam said, happily, "Sounds good. Make it two."

The bartender said, "You got it," and eyeballed me. Then he said, "Hey, you're the guy that was with Dennis Wilson the last night he was here."

Confused, Sam asked, "You were in here with Dennis Wilson?"

I explained, "I picked Dennis up near the Santa Monica pier and gave him a ride here a couple of days before I left for New York. We had some mai tais, and then he really lost it, man. When the bartender kicked him out of here, he decided to march across the street to the motel to see his 18-year-old wife. He jaywalked through rush-hour traffic, totally oblivious to screeching brakes and honking cars."

"Whoa, man, sounds like Dennis was really hitting bottom."

Sam said, sadly.

The bartender was within earshot, and he continued my story. "Yeah, he was on his last leg. It was *really* bad. He'd been beat up just the night before you were in here with him. And to think Dennis was once 'Mr. Hollywood.'"

"Well, that explains the cuts and scratches all over his face and arms. I'd wondered what the hell happened to him," I sighed.

"Wow. Mr. Hollywood. This whole thing is a tragedy." Sam said.

"After you both left, he stumbled back in here about twenty minutes later, covered in blood. One eye was completely swollen shut and he could barely walk. I told him I couldn't allow him in here in his condition. He was almost crazy—he jumped up, grabbed me around the neck, started choking me, and yelled, 'Just give me a drink, asshole. I'm Dennis Wilson of the Beach Boys and I made this fucking bar!'"

He continued, "Another guy recognized Dennis and told me, 'I got it. Put it on my tab.' The guy pulled a clean T-shirt from his beach bag, handed it to Dennis, and bought him a couple more mai tais.

"He came back around here once more, but he was too out of it for me to let him in. We never saw him again after that. Sadly, he drowned a month later. It was a shocking tragedy. A Beach Boy—a surfer—*drowning*, of all things. Dennis Wilson of the Beach Boys. I can hardly believe it. He had everything; he led a charmed life."

Shaking his head in dismay, he added, "Who would have ever thought that would be his fate? Drowning in fifteen feet of water right here in Marina Del Rey before he even reached the age of forty. And he never *did* pay his bar tab."

THE CAMEL MAN

When we finished our drinks, Sam asked, "So, where are you going to stay, Rock?"

"I have no idea. I was wondering if you knew anybody who might be looking for a roommate or has a spare couch, just until I can put something together."

"Man, are you lucky. My roommate just split for two months. You got any money?"

"Some. How much would you charge me for rent, Sam?"

Sam pondered the situation for a minute, "Well, look, I need a roommate and you need a place to stay, so let's just make it an even $300. We're beach pals and it's just temporary. That'll still leave you some breathing room. I'm not worried about it. You're like a cat with nine lives—you always land on your feet."

"Done! Thanks, Sam, you're the best." We shook hands on it.

Sam's Brentwood condo was pretty nice, and we had a lot in common. He had been a pole vaulter at UCLA around the same time I went to Oregon, and we were both beach people.

I called my agent the next day and told him I was back in town and ready to start auditioning. In a few days, I landed a commercial for Chevy Lumina. Ka-ching! I also resumed classes with the famed acting coach Milton Katselas, who had won the best director Oscar in 1968 for Goldie Hawn's first movie, *Butterflies are Free*.

That took care of business and improving myself, and I was ready for my love life to catch up with my acting and modeling career.

I always talked to Stephen regularly during this time. He had long since been estranged from the Beach Boys, and I remember once asking him if he had kept in touch with Al Jardine since they'd been such good friends.

Stephen had helped Al become a partner in Brother Records

with Carl and Dennis; that helped give Al some extra security as a band member. In fact, Al became the President of Brother Records and he was given an equal share and a full vote.

Al had a beautiful voice, long blond hair, the quintessential Beach Boys' look, and he was a terrific rhythm guitar player to boot. His steady playing style freed up Carl to explore his fabulous solo guitar talent.

Al was always close with Mike Love and followed Mike's lead into becoming a transcendental meditator. It turned out that Stephen had kept in touch with Al, but there was a cooling of their relationship because of the big issues that had been in play during some of the bumpier times.

A couple of years later, I started dating singer Rita Coolidge, Kris Kristofferson's ex-wife. Rita experienced a tidal wave of fame and attention in 1977 with her smash hit, "(Your Love Has Lifted Me) Higher and Higher." In 1983, she was chosen to sing one of the classic James Bond movie theme songs, "All Time High," for *Octopussy*.

Rita and I met at a party at Joanna Carson's house. Joanna, who was Johnny Carson's ex-wife, introduced me to a group that included Rita, Jon Voight, Edward James Olmos, and Lou Gossett. Out of nowhere, Rita asked Jon, "Do you think Kris can act?"

Though Voight seemed a bit taken aback by the question, he managed to recover diplomatically, "Well, let's put it this way. He's got *something*." The others nodded in agreement, but the moment still felt a little awkward.

I smiled at Rita. "It's called *star power*."

Jon said, "That's a good way of putting it."

Rita and I began dating. Early in our relationship, we went to New Orleans, where she'd help set up a benefit concert for the homeless. She and her friends performed, including Linda Ronstadt, Bonnie Raitt, Jimmy Buffett, Aaron Neville and some others.

We had a good time in the Big Easy—everyone was relaxed, having fun, and joking around. At one point, a group was rehearsing harmonies backstage before the performance as Aaron Neville was struggling to fasten his bow tie. He was a gigantic guy with a 19-inch neck, too musclebound to reach behind his neck and fasten the clasp. Though he was surrounded by singing women, it didn't occur to any of them to help him.

The inspiration I gained working with The Beach Boys helped me launch an extraordinary career. Here I am with Steve Love (left) in Hawaii celebrating my landing the "International Camel Man" campaign job. I was on top of the world.

Photo by and courtesy of Sandra Ficalora

I finally walked over, said, "Here, let me give you a hand," and fastened the tie clasp for him. We posed cheek-by-cheek and got a small round of applause.

Being backstage brought back good memories of touring with the Beach Boys, and I felt at home. I missed the guys—Mike's energy, Brian's sweetness, even Dennis' hammering on the drums and breaking drumsticks right and left. Being on the inside and helping to watch over Brian may have been stressful, but it sure had its moments.

The concert was a big success, and the money it raised

helped a lot of distressed people in that storm-ravaged city. When it was over, Rita and I left to meet Linda Ronstadt for dinner in the French Quarter at K-Paul's Louisiana Kitchen, the Cajun/Creole restaurant owned by the celebrity chef Paul Prudhomme. On the way to the restaurant, we smoked a joint in the limo as we sang the last tune from the show, "I-ko, I-ko," a Cajun bayou ditty that went like this:

Talk-in' 'bout, hey now! Hey now! I-ko, I-ko, un-day Jock-a-mo fee-no ai na-né, jock-a-mo fee na-né.

It was silliness, to be sure, but it was fun. I loved it.

A few months later, Stephen made one of his rare visits to the mainland from his surfing paradise on Kauai. We got together at Rita's house in the Hollywood Hills to watch the 1990 Grammy awards. It was fun watching Linda Ronstadt win a couple of awards; Rita and I were whooping and yelling for her and Neville when they won the Grammy for "Best Vocal Performance by a Pop Group or Duo."

Seeing Stephen so soon after the New Orleans concert triggered some intense memories of my times with the Beach Boys. I was surprised how sad I became when I thought of Dennis and our crazy history. The last time I saw him, he was wading out into hazardous traffic, drunk, drug-addled, hopeless, and heading for trouble. Though there was nothing I could have done to stop him, I felt a pang of regret for all his wasted talent.

A few weeks after Stephen returned to Hawaii, I auditioned for the International Camel Man role, a highly lucrative multi-year endorsement deal. This was a big deal—a *big* job, the kind of job that makes a modeling career, not to mention lots of moolah. Of the thousands of male models who auditioned from around the world, only 996 were videotaped. I answered seven callbacks.

The Camel Man

Steve Love doing what he still loves best, surfing off the shore of his beloved Hanalei Bay in Kauai, Hawaii. This photo was taken in 1980 two years after he parted ways with The Beach Boys after being their manager throughout the 70's.
Photo by Lee Lucas
Courtesy of Steve Love

On May 1st, 1990, a date that just happened to be Rita's birthday, I got the call from my agent at William Morris. I waited until that evening at Rita's star-studded birthday party to share my momentous news.

Rita opened my present, a crystal dolphin, kissed me and told me she loved it. I couldn't hold it in any longer, so I whispered in her ear, "I got the Camel Man job!"

Rita smiled. "I *told* you I'd bring you good luck." I guess that was her way of congratulating me (or perhaps taking credit).

That evening, I chatted with Rita's close friend Joanna

Carson, at whose home I'd met Rita the year before. I told Joanna I'd been asked to submit a brief biography to R.J. Reynolds, the company that owns the Camel brand. In the bio, I'd said that my girlfriend, Rita Coolidge, brought me good luck.

When everyone was gone, Rita complained, "I can't believe you used my name in a bio. I'm not a trophy!"

I couldn't believe my ears. "I simply mentioned that you brought me good luck, the very same thing *you* said when I told you I got the job."

To my amazement, Rita continued to harangue me about what she felt was an indiscretion. Finally, I'd had enough. "You know what? You're absolutely right. You're *not* a trophy, and you know what else you're not? You're not being very nice on what is supposed to be a big night for me as well."

That was it for me. I was gone.

The first Camel Man shoot took place in New Guinea and lasted five weeks. A provision in my contract allowed me to bring an assistant or companion who'd travel first class with me and receive a per diem allowance of $150. What a nice perk that was! I had planned to take Rita with me, but I decided to take my dad instead. Jim had been stationed in New Guinea during World War II as a Marine Corps pilot, flying in fuel from the Philippines.

When word got out about my travel perks, I had friends I didn't even know I knew. They came out of the woodwork and were standing in line to travel first class around the world to exotic places: Hong Kong, Singapore, Kuala Lumpur, Bermuda, Bahamas, Jamaica, Malaysia, Dominica, Australia, New Guinea, Hawaii, Puerto Rico, and Borneo.

I had unbelievable adventures as the Camel Man. In Malaysia, my little boat capsized and lost the engine while I

The Camel Man

was crossing a raging river. I floated downstream for a couple of miles before our helicopter could hoist me out of the river with a rope—and there were crocodiles everywhere.

The adventures continued in the States. We shot a sequence near Colorado Springs, where I hung precariously off a 14,000-foot cliff for an entire week. I'll admit—I was scared shitless.

I was living large at this point in my life—bought a new Mercedes with my early wages, and, a year later, sank a bundle of dough into an English Tudor house in Westwood. I gave Stephen and a dear college football buddy, Steve "Bones" Reina, a week-long, all-expenses paid vacation in Hawaii. We had a blast in my old stomping grounds, and it was one of the best weeks of my life.

Life in general was the proverbial bowl of cherries for the next two-and-a-half years. Things started to go bad when I learned that Bones had leukemia and needed chemotherapy. The very next night, the cherries spoiled. I saw on the news that R.J. Reynolds lost a class-action lawsuit, suffering a whopping $138-million-dollar adverse judgment.

I got on the phone to the R.J. Reynolds CEO, and I asked when we were going out on location again. The response I got was not what I wanted to hear: "We don't have any immediate plans for further filming at the present." Not good! Not good at all.

Thanks to the tobacco company's financial woes, eventually I got the official word that my Camel Man promotional campaign was, alas, suspended. On that same day, I got the far more tragic news that my dear friend Bones, whom I loved like a brother, died. I felt like howling, but not the happy howls of my Brian era.

Chapter Twenty-Seven

Thanks!

My phone rang, waking me up at 11 a.m. on a Saturday. "Who's calling me at this ungodly hour?" I answered sleepily.

"Hey, big daddy!" I didn't recognize the caller's voice, though it sounded familiar.

"Who *is* this?" I pressed.

"What's happening, big daddy?"

"*Brian?*"

"Yeah, man. What's happening, Daddy-o?"

"Uh, well . . . you tell *me*, man. I didn't think you were talking to me." It was mid-1979, six months since I'd worked for him.

"Why don't you come over?" Brian cheerfully answered.

This invite surprised me. "Who's there with you?"

"Just someone who takes care of things. Come on over," Brian insisted.

Stunned, stalling for time to think, I asked, "You're in a new place on Greentree, right?"

"Yeah," Brian confirmed.

"All right, I know where it is. Stan drove me by one time."

"How soon can you get here?

"I've just got to jump in the shower."

"You can jump in the Jacuzzi here," Brian countered.

"Is it hot?"

"Yeah, it's hot."

"Give me five."

"Don't give me no jive," Brian said, good-naturedly.

"If I'm lyin', I'm dyin'," and I hung up.

Immediately, I called Stan at his other house in Laguna, where he was staying with his girlfriend. "You won't believe who just called me!"

"Who?"

"You'll never guess."

After a long pause, Stan somehow guessed, "Brian?"

I was shocked. "How the hell did you guess that?"

"Something about how excited you were. What did he say?"

"He said, 'What's happening, Big Daddy?' You're not gonna believe this—he wants me to come over."

"You're kidding."

"I swear to God. I can't believe it!"

"I don't fucking believe it either. He doesn't call *me*!"

There was absolute silence for five seconds. "All right, listen. Why don't you come up from Laguna and meet me at Brian's? I'll tell him I called you and told you to come over."

"Okay, I'll see you at Brian's in an hour." He hung up.

Brian's new pad was a cool, white Mediterranean stucco job, tucked away at the end of a cul-de-sac, snuggled into a remote Palisades hillside forest. The front door was open, and Brian was pacing back and forth from the door to a pale blue Cadillac parked in the driveway. He was barefoot, drinking a beer, and when he saw me, he sang out, "Let's get back together and do it again."

Thanks!

When I got out of my car, he rushed over and hugged me affectionately, accidentally spilling some of his beer onto my shirt. "Hey, big daddy!"

I laughed, "Well, I might as well have a beer if I'm gonna wear one, eh, Brian?"

"Yeah, it ain't a party till someone spills a beer!" He turned around, left me at the front entrance, went inside, walked into the kitchen, came back to the living room with a cold Coors in his hand, and held it out to me.

Sensing that it wasn't necessary to be formally invited, I walked into the house. "Well, I guess it's officially a party, then!"

When Brian asked if I still played the piano, I was glad to be able to say I was. "Yeah, those inversions you showed me when I first started working for you really helped me learn to play."

"Play me something."

I took a big pull off the Coors, carefully set it down on a coaster, sat down at the black upright piano facing the front door, and played "Imagine." This was my standard warmup piece. Brian stood there looking down at my hands, broke into a broad grin, then sang along on the choruses. When I finished the song, he said, "You play with feeling, Rocky."

Brian got us a couple of more beers. It sure wasn't the way things went down when Stan and I had been around, but there wasn't anything I could do about it. It didn't feel right.

"Play something else." Brian said, as he started pacing around the room.

Never needing much urging, I played "California Girls." Brian continued to pace—and drink.

"Not bad, Rocky. You *did* learn the inversions. Keep playing."

I played "Darlin" and "Surfer Girl." Brian continued to pace with his ear cocked sort of sideways and upwards. He was listening intently, and he sang harmony on all the choruses.

I was extremely flattered. Brian never ever sings along with anyone unless he likes what he's hearing. Then I switched to an Elton John's song, "Tiny Dancer," which has an intricate lead-in. After a minute, Brian walked up to the piano on my left, put his left hand on the piano, said, "Add the "G" in the bass," and demonstrated the chord.

"I knew something was missing," I said, and rehearsed the bass a couple times. I played the song as Brian paced around the room in circles, drinking his beer.

When I finished, Brian said, "That's pretty good. How'd you learn the intro?"

"From the sheet music. I wrote down the individual notes." It had taken forever to learn it. Next, I played the Beatles' "Let It Be." I was running out of songs. Brian was singing harmony on the chorus, when there was a knock on the open door, and in walked Stan.

I quickly explained, "I called Stan and told him to come over and join us. You don't mind, do ya, B.W.?"

Stan said, "Eh, Brian."

Brian smiled, "Eh, Stan," and started pacing again.

I continued to play "Let It Be." When I got to the chorus, I was hopeful that Brian would start singing again. On the second refrain, Brian did. "Let it be, let it be, let it be, yeah, let it be. Crystal words of wisdom, let it be."

After I finished the song, Brian said, poignantly, "Crystal words of wisdom, *let's* let it be." The three of us laughed. It felt like old times again. Brian's words were damn appropriate.

Brian suddenly blurted, "Yeah, you guys really saved my ass."

THANKS!

"Hear that, Stan?" I asked softly. "I take that as a 'thanks.' How about you?"

"Yeah, I'd say that was a 'thanks.'" Stan looked genuinely moved.

We moved to the back patio. It had great landscaping—a stone wall with a barbeque, an eight-foot-high natural rock waterfall, pond, and Jacuzzi—backing up to an aromatic pine forest.

I quickly took full advantage of the spa.

"Do you use your Jacuzzi, Brian?" I asked.

"Are you kidding? First thing every morning, just like we used to do. I don't get to play basketball anymore, though," he said a little wistfully.

"This is great, Brian. I love the waterfall. I love the sound of it! There's nothing like the sound of a waterfall."

"Yeah, that's the main thing I love about this place, the waterfall and the soothing sound."

The three of us spent the afternoon relaxing and reminiscing. Brian's caregiver cooked a few burgers, beers were flowing, and laughter filled the pine-scented air. Then, typically, without saying anything, Brian slipped away to take a nap. Stan and I left.

When we got back to our Palisades house, we high-fived each other without saying a word. Clearly, we each felt a sense of inner satisfaction.

I spoke first. "Brian never ceases to amaze me."

Stan shook his head. "I know what you mean. This takes the cake, though."

"I actually think he loves us, Stan."

Stan conceded, "Maybe."

I mused aloud, "I still can't believe Brian called me."

"I know, I can't believe it either. He didn't call me and *I'm* his cousin."

"You know the part I'll never forget? When Brian said, 'Crystal words of wisdom, *let's* let it be,' and the three of us laughed. I felt we bonded again. That was, without a doubt, the defining moment for me."

"You know what, Rocky? You're right. That was a great moment. I'm glad I walked in on 'Let It Be;' it was the perfect song for me to walk in on. You and I worked hard to protect Brian and keep him alive. Deep down, I think he *does* love us."

Chapter Twenty-Eight

You Know It's True— Brian's Back

The next Saturday was a clear, sunny day. I was enjoying a cup of steaming hot Kona coffee as I sat at my piano, playing and singing a song I was trying to write.

A car honked, and it sounded like it was right in front of my house. I looked outside and saw a baby blue Cadillac convertible pulled in sideways across the bottom of my steep driveway. Brian was at the wheel.

I couldn't believe my eyes—Brian, two weeks in a row— and *driving*. In all our years together, I'd never seen him behind the wheel. I ambled outside, coffee mug in hand, barefoot, and walked down the driveway.

"So, *I'm* not the only one who goes around barefoot," Brian laughed.

I grinned, "No, *you're* the only one who gets on a plane going to Minnesota in the dead of winter, barefoot."

"Jump in," Brian said.

"Where're we going?"

"Does it matter?"

I laughed. "Not really."

"Up the coast," Brian revealed.

"Up the coast is good. So, you drive now?"

"Yeah."

I was suspicious. "You got a license?

Brian nodded. "Yeah."

"Show me!"

Brian pulled a single laminated item from his left shirt pocket. It was his California driver's license, all right.

I shook my head and smiled. "*Damn*, bro, you're legit." I vaulted over the passenger door and slid into the shotgun seat. As we cruised down Chautauqua to Pacific Coast Highway and turned north, I asked, "So when did you get your license?

"Couple of weeks ago," Brian said breezily.

"How long did you go without driving?"

"The lady at the DMV said it'd been ten years."

We rode in silence for a while. I wasn't sure what the vibe was yet.

"So, what was that you were playing when I pulled up?" Brian asked.

"That was 'You Know it's True.'"

"Is it yours?"

"Yeah, but I don't know if it's any good."

Brian offered some advice. "Don't judge it. Just say what you feel." Then he sang my song, just as I'd sung it a couple of minutes before:

"*I need you, darlin',*
You know it's true.
I would do anything
To have you."

You Know It's True—Brian's Back

So, what's next?"

I was astonished that Brian was interested in my song. I sang:

"I've waited so long,
For your love.
Say that it's me, girl,
Say that it's us."

Brian asked, "Is there a chorus?"

I sang the chorus:

"It feels so real,
I can't explain,
It feels so real,
Tell me you feel the same."

Brian smiled. "I like it! Go on."

I shook my head. "That's all I got so far."

"So, who's the song about?"

"It's about a girl I knew when I was in college."

"The white t-shirt chick?" Brian mused.

"No, *not* the white t-shirt chick," I chuckled. "I made that up, Brian. The whole white t-shirt chick thing!"

"Rocky! You made up the white t-shirt chick?" Brian exclaimed, disappointment in his voice.

"Yeah, it was just to get you to laugh, you know, when I first met you. Sorry, Brian."

"So, there's no white t-shirt chick? Damn, it was so funny! You tricked me." Brian threw his head back and let go with one of his huge belly laughs.

"So, let me ask you something, Brian. Why did you call me?"

"I called you to let you know there is no problem between us," Brian said simply.

"Well, I'm really glad. That means a lot to me, and I have to admit I was really surprised to see you sitting in your car in my driveway today."

Brian teased, "You're not gonna get all sappy on me now, are ya?"

I reached over and turned up the volume on the radio as we drove up the coast and sang along to the Rascal's old hit single, "Groovin'."

Brian and I sang all the way up the coast to Pt. Mugu, Malibu, where we parked his Caddy and walked along the coastline for almost an hour, chatting about nothing in particular. Some of the time, we just walked in silence.

As we walked, I thought to myself about how I had always been more quiet and thoughtful around Brian, which was not my usual style. Though I'm outspoken and widely known as a tough guy, something about Brian and his innate sweetness awakened some new emotions in me. Even if I *had* thrashed the other Wilson brothers pretty thoroughly over the past few years, I knew those episodes had been triggered by my protective instincts. I'd become a kinder, gentler version of myself. Brian changed me for the better.

We were comfortable with each other. We did some reminiscing, some frank confessions, some storytelling—but we shed no tears. Mostly, there were lots of laughs. Brian was the most relaxed I had ever seen him. I felt honored.

When we got back to Brian's car, I shook my head in disbelief. "I still can't believe you're driving, man. That's great, Brian. So, you're, uh, okay?"

Brian gave me his crooked smile, and said, "Yeah, I'm okay, Rocky. You don't have to worry about me anymore."

"Well, I'm proud of you, Brian. It seems you've taken your

You Know It's True—Brian's Back

life back." Then I couldn't stop myself from adding, "I don't know about all that beer drinking last weekend."

Brian ignored that, and said, triumphantly, "Yeah, I *am* taking my life back! Hey—you, Stan, and Stephen saved my ass! I'M BAAACK!"

Throwing my head back and letting go with a big belly laugh of my own, I yelled Stephen's slogan, "Brian's back!"

Brian chimed in with me, "Brian's back!" and together we sang out *"Brian's back!"* filling the air as we rolled on down Pacific Coast Highway singing and laughing our asses off.

Brian said jovially, "We're cruisin'."

As I began to trust Brian's driving and really relax, I realized how I surprised I was to see him at my house today, especially behind the wheel.

I looked over at Brian, but he was focused on the road.

I had to admit, he seemed at peace with himself. Brian was taking his life back. I felt a twang. I'd never seem him so in charge, so *grown up*. Think of it—Brian was only 19 years old when he was hit by a tidal wave of fame. He was so young when his normal life ended.

Stan and had I poured our hearts and soul into saving Brian. We watched him evolve, watched him come back to reality and start to enjoy life again. He had been changing and becoming a man, maybe for the first time. Now it looked like he'd finally made it all the way without us.

We headed back to the Palisades. Brian was at the wheel, the wind was in his hair, and he started to sing, "I need you, darlin'. . ."

I was amazed that he remembered my song. As I smiled and joined him, harmonizing, "You know it's true," I thought to myself, "Brian is the sweetest yet most enigmatic person I have ever known."

While it was gratifying that Brian had reached out to me—the song fest and cookout at his house and our cruise up the coast to Malibu were, for sure, the highlight of my summer—I never followed up. I could have dropped by his pad, as he invited me to do, or called him. I thought about it, and I often wanted to see him and talk to him.

I found that I couldn't do it.

Stephen, Stan, and I had worked too hard to keep Brian drug- and alcohol-free. Something about his partying just didn't feel right, even if it maybe was just beer.

As much as I still love him, and as much as I have always dug hanging out with him, I knew *I* couldn't be the person who was drinking with him. I decided then that I wasn't going be like his brother, Dennis—I was not going to be an enabler. If that meant I couldn't have the pleasure of his company, then, regretfully, I needed to stay away.

I had *no* regrets about any of my actions in the two-and-a-half years I was with Brian 24/7. I know without a doubt that Stephen, Stan, and I saved his life. I'd seen Brian at his worst as we helped him recover from his decade-long wipeout, and I knew how far he'd come since then. After seeing him those two weekends, I understood that Brian had rebooted his long-interrupted task of growing up. Early fame stunts many young lives, and his was no exception.

It took Brian a few years to finish the growing up process, especially when he was interrupted again by the now-infamous Dr. Landy. When he found Melinda Ledbetter, who rescued him from Landy's clutches a second time and became his wife, all of us who loved him knew the truth: Brian was finally, fully back.

·

About the Authors

Rushton "Rocky" Pamplin

Also known as Rush, Rocky has had a colorful and often controversial life. He's known for his dangerous combination of knock-em-dead good looks and a sizzling hot temper. Though Rocky thrived on beach and party life, he was always a star athlete. At University of Oregon on a football scholarship, he roomed with future NBA first-round draft pick Stan Love and befriended his brother Stephen, a Beach Boys manager.

Drafted by the New Orleans Saints in 1971, Rocky was plagued with injuries in the pros. His acting and modeling career took off in 1975, and in 1976 his famous Playgirl centerfold was published. Major ad campaigns included a Wheaties commercial and cereal box cover, the Winston Man campaign, and a several-year stint as the International Camel Man. Rocky has also acted, including in The Young and the Restless in 1985-86, sung on several albums, and he writes music. He lives in the Los Angeles area.

Ron Hamady

About Ron Hamady: Ron has been immersed in music since he managed the R&B singing group Bloodstone, best known for their platinum-selling album Natural High. Although he came from Flint, Michigan, deep in the heart of Motown county, Ron has loved the gorgeous harmonies and infectious music of the Beach Boys since he was a teenager.

Ron's perspective as a feature film producer, writer, director, and member of the Academy of Motion Picture Arts and Sciences gives him a uniquely insightful view into the workings of the Beach Boys. His collaboration with Rocky Pamplin reveals previously untold stories about America's Band and why it's still going strong, 55 years into a great American love story.

www.ingramcontent.com/pod-product-compliance
Lightning Source LLC
Chambersburg PA
CBHW030231170426
43201CB00006B/183